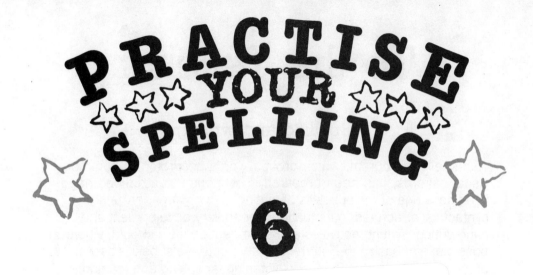

6

John Rose

© Copp Clark Longman Ltd., 1994.
Pearson Education Canada, Inc., Toronto, Ontario

Editors: Evlyn Windross, Marion Elliott, Grace D'Alfonso
Cover Design: Rob McPhail
Cover Illustration: Marie-Louise Gay

ISBN 0-7730-5430-8

Copp Clark Longman Ltd.

Printed and bound in Canada

8 9 -WC- 03 02

To the Teacher

Spelling and writing

This spelling program, which groups words according to common visual patterns, has been prepared in response to a defined need. Spelling is one of the subskills of writing, along with appropriate syntactical structures, punctuation, vocabulary development and handwriting. Writing activities at the elementary level should, wherever possible, emphasize the interrelationship of these subskills as well as of the other areas of language — listening, speaking and reading.

It is important for children to have the desire and ability to express, through writing, their ideas, thoughts, feelings and knowledge with increasing confidence and skill.

Spelling ability grows most effectively when viewed as an integral part of the total language program and developed through a continuous program which recognizes both increasing ability and changing interests of the writer. As children develop the desire to communicate their ideas in writing, they need skills in spelling that can be provided systematically. The skills and the appropriate experiences can, in many instances, go hand in hand.

How to use this book

This book contains forty units, four of which are review units. Each of the thirty-six main units begins with a list of words that contain a common visual element. Several activities in the unit are related to these list words; there is also a variety of more general activities: word hunts, puzzles, crosswords, etc.

There are many ways of treating the list words as they are introduced. One possible approach, in five stages, is described below. A stage may represent a day's lesson, or two or three stages may be covered in one day.

Stage 1: Introduction

Introduce the element (e.g. *ar* words) to the children and point it out as a visual element found in all of the words in that grouping. At the same time go through the list of words ensuring that the children are familiar with the meanings, and identify the common visual element in each word.

Stage 2: Look Cover Think Write Check

Each child is asked to perform these five tasks:

Look: The child looks at a particular word in the list and 'spells' the word silently. This should not be done letter by letter (e.g. s–h–o–u–l–d–e–r) but should be broken up into meaningful elements (sh–ould–er).

Cover: The word is simply covered by another book, ruler, etc.

Think: The child must think about the covered word before attempting to write it; for example, what is the 'structure' of the word? What is the element contained in the word?

Write: The word is written out.

Check: The child checks to see whether his or her spelling is correct. If a mistake has been made, the child should write out the word in full again and should not, for example, merely put in a letter that has been omitted.

Stage 3: Extension

As the majority of the words in this book have been presented in their base form, this stage extends them by adding prefixes, suffixes and inflectional endings, and by changing tense (where the element is not changed) and writing plural forms.

Stage 4: Writing applications

As spelling is a subskill of writing, the words the children are working with (both the list words and the extensions) are now used in as many different writing situations as possible. In addition to those in this book, these may include writing poetry such as couplets, free verse, triangular poems, alliterative poems, etc., advertisements, jingles, short stories, posters, newspaper reports, greetings for cards, messages, definitions, captions and labels, riddles, jokes, puzzles, etc.

Stage 5: Evaluation and review

At this stage the children are asked to spell a number of words in a 'test' situation. The words may be either list words or extensions of those words and could be from the unit currently being taught as well as the two previous units. Using this approach the words are continually being reviewed. In addition, there is some degree of built-in review in that some words appear in more than one list; for example, *shadow* may be in both the *sh* and *ow* words.

Contents

Unit 1

a–e words

> decorate celebrate parade climate chocolate
> replace taste waste separate language

1 Write each of the list words in your book. Use each one in a sentence of your own.

2 Fill the blanks in the sentences with words from the list.

  a The area around Kamloops has a fairly warm _____.

  b The new student from Vietnam is trying very hard to learn the English _____.

  c Rosa helped her mother to _____ the white clothes from the coloured ones before she did the washing.

  d Can you _____ the orange flavour in the icing?

  e Over a dozen bands are marching in the _____ .

  f Industrial _____ must be prevented from polluting our rivers.

  g Jewish people _____ a holiday known as Yom Kippur by fasting and going to the synagogue.

  h Luke and Kelly love to _____ the Christmas tree.

  i Would you please _____ those books on the shelf?

  j Julie gave me a _____ bar on my birthday.

More a–e Words

3 Here are some more **a–e** words. Find their meanings in a dictionary and write each word with its meaning in your own book.

charade	facade	promenade	arcade
serenade	cascade	stockade	bale
accolade	barricade	impale	deliberat e

4 Write three list words that can be made from these letters:

E T A C O R E C E L H S E R L O A P A E T P A C

Vertical Words

5 Use the clues to find these seven-letter words. When you have finished, the first column down will give you one of the list words.

a A piece of furniture for holding ornamental objects or papers. The same word can mean a chosen number of ministers who govern a country

b A large wild animal of the cat family with a spotted skin

c A kind of printing that slopes to the right (*as these words do*)

d An afternoon performance of a show

e A tar mixture used to make a smooth hard surface on roads and paths

f The loud crashing or rumbling noise heard after a flash of lightning

g To put to death by law

6 Use the clues to complete each word.

a A paste made from the ground-up seeds of the cocoa tree; a sweet _ _ _ _ _ _ _ a _ e

b To mark a special occasion by entertainment, festivities, etc. _ _ _ _ _ _ _ a _ e

c Not connected; to go different ways _ _ _ _ _ _ _ a _ e

d A distinct variety of speech used in a country (such as English, French, Chinese, etc.) _ _ _ _ _ _ a _ e

e The weather conditions of a region _ _ _ _ _ a _ e

f To make something look beautiful _ _ _ _ _ a _ e

g To use up or spend carelessly _ a _ _ _ e

h To put back _ _ _ _ _ a _ e

i A procession of people, sometimes in costume; also an orderly arrangement of troops for inspection _ _ _ a _ e

Number Words — Words Meaning One

7   **a**   Which **uni** word means one of a kind?   uni _ _ _

     b   Which **uni** word means to have the same clothing; to be dressed alike?   uni _ _ _ _

     c   Which **mono** word means complete control over something?   mono _ _ _ _

     d   Which **mono** word means a king or leader? mon _ _ _ _

     e   Which **uni** word is a mythical animal?   uni _ _ _ _ _

     f   Which **uni** word means to sing together as one? uni _ _ _

     g   Which **uni** word means an educational institution? uni _ _ _ _ _ _ _

     h   Which **uni** word means the whole of creation? uni _ _ _ _ _

     i   Which **uni** word means a one-wheeled vehicle? uni _ _ _ _ _

     j   Which **mono** word means shades of one colour? mono _ _ _ _ _ _

     k   Which **mono** word means a design using one's initials? mono _ _ _ _

     l   Which **mono** word means singing on one note? mono _ _ _ _

Word Diamonds

8   Use the clues to complete this puzzle.

Across:
2   Nervous in the company of others; bashful
4   Fed up with continual dull talk
5   A large passenger-carrying vehicle

Down:
1   A small, low bush
2   To breathe while weeping
3   Opposite of no

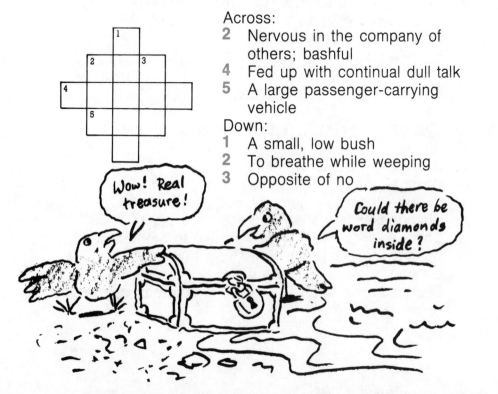

Unit 2

> scene   mere   stampede   hemisphere   complete
> athlete   concrete   compete   sincere   recede

1 Write each of the list words in your book. Use each one in a sentence of your own.

2 Use the clues to complete each word.

   a Genuine; free from deceit or falseness
      _ _ _ _ e _ e

   b A sudden rush of frightened animals
      _ _ _ _ _ e _ e

   c A view of a place. Also the background for the action of a play   _ _ e _ e

   d A person skilled at games needing strength and speed   _ _ _ _ e _ e

   e Finished; with nothing missing   _ _ _ _ _ e _ e

   f Half of the earth or half of a globe representing the earth   _ _ _ _ _ _ _ _ e _ e

   g To strive with others to gain something, for example, in a race for a prize   _ _ _ _ _ e _ e

   h To move or go back; to become more distant
      _ _ _ e _ e

   i Simply; only   _ e _ e

   j A mixture of cement, gravel, etc.   _ _ _ _ _ _ e _ e

Anagrams

3 **a** Change <u>cones</u> into a hot buttered biscuit.
   b Change <u>votes</u> into something found in the kitchen.
   c Change <u>livers</u> into a metal.
   d Change <u>lose</u> into the bottom part of a shoe.
   e Change <u>flog</u> into a game played on a course.
   f Change <u>flow</u> into a wild animal.
   g Change <u>cares</u> into a word meaning to frighten or bully.
   h Change <u>sleep</u> into the skins from fruit.
   i Change <u>gnat</u> into a sharp taste.
   j Change <u>cause</u> into something put on meat, vegetables or pasta.

'S' Words

4

a	S						
b		S					
c			S				
d				S			
e					S		
f						S	
g							S
h						S	
i					S		
j				S			
k			S				
l		S					
m	S						

a A small, swift-flying bird with a deeply forked-tail
b Feeling uncomfortable because you have done something wrong
c A sudden, vigorous attack
d Can be stretched and then returns to its own shape
e A flower, especially of a plant which produces fruit
f To use up or to fire out. Also the pipe from an engine which lets out waste gas, steam, etc.
g Extremely angry or violent
h A speech given to an audience. Also the name or number of a house, street, town, etc. where a person lives

i A deep red colour, tinged with blue
j Buildings where criminals are kept locked up for varying periods of time
k A long narrow way between rooms in a building. Also a journey on a ship
l A very large, long-legged bird which cannot fly but is able to run swiftly
m To stroll along without hurrying

Word Puzzle

5

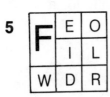

How many words of four letters or more can you make from the letters in the box? Each word must contain the large letter, and each letter can be used only once in each word.

6 Complete these sentences with list words.
  a The _____ won two gold medals at the Olympics.
  b Canada is situated in the northern _____.
  c The criminal returned to the _____ of the crime.
  d Three horses were killed in the _____.
  e The floodwaters began to _____ after four days.
  f The convict made a _____ effort to reform.
  g It's nothing much, just a _____ trinket.
  h The athletes will _____ at the next Olympics.
  i The library has a _____ set of books by Eric Wilson.
  j The road was paved with _____.

Fits to a 'T'

7 Use the clues to find these words that all end in **T**

a	R					T
b	R					T
c	R					T
d	R					T
e	R					T
f	R					T
g	R					T
h	R					T
i	R					T
j	R					T

And now...

  a A small furry, burrowing animal with long ears
  b To take notes of some happening, especially for a newspaper
  c A loud and continued noise; an uproar
  d To say or do something again
  e The outcome of some action, for example, a horse race
  f A missile projected into the sky by a backward jet of hot gases
  g A rebellion
  h A short time ago
  i A person who rules in place of a king or queen
  j Strong, healthy, vigorous

Unit 3

o–e words

suppose   telescope   microscope   drone   zone
chrome   revoke   strove   cope   elope

1 Write each of the list words in your book. Use each one in a sentence of your own.

2 Fill the blanks in these sentences with list words.

a   Most of the world's wheat is grown in the North Temperate _____.

b   Kathy couldn't concentrate on her work because she was distracted by the low _____ of the machine outside.

c   In the film, the girl climbed down the ladder to _____ with the boy next door.

d   Car lovers often have a lot of _____ around the engines.

e   When I got home from school Mom said, 'I _____ you're hungry?'

f   General Custer's soldiers _____ against overwhelming odds.

g   Captain Cook first saw the east coast of Australia through a _____.

h   A manager has to _____ with many business problems every day.

i   The insect was so small you needed a _____ to see it.

j   The police will _____ your licence if you get caught speeding again.

3 Circle the words that have the same or similar meaning to the list word.

a   *drone* — talk, waffle, compute, gabble, gable

b   *zone* — sing, region, locality, district, alien

c   *revoke* — revolt, quash, dance, repeal, cancel

d   *strove* — struggled, strained, exerted, toiled, rested

e   *elope* — antelope, deer, wed, marriage, moose

4 Match the list word with the correct definition.

a *Suppose* means
— a stocking that stays up by itself
— to show off; to put on an act
— consider as true; to take as likely
— to prevent from appearing

b *Drone* means
— a continuous dull low sound
— a male bee
— both of the above
— none of the above

c A *zone* is
— a type of large tropical lizard
— a division or an area
— the point in the heavens directly overhead
— a bluish-white metal

d *Revoke* means
— to end; to cancel
— to act violently against those in power
— a punishment given in return for harm done
— to avoid company

e *Strove* means
— something you cook on in a kitchen
— to row quickly in a small boat
— to strike with a weapon
— to have struggled hard

f *Elope* means
— to walk slowly for pleasure
— to run away secretly to get married
— a type of African antelope
— a safety-lamp for miners

5 Find the **o—e words.**

		O		E
a		O		E
b		O		E
c		O		E
d		O		E
e		O		E
f		O		E
g		O		E
h		O		E
i		O		E
j		O		E

a Fur or cloth worn over the shoulders and hanging down
b To put fuel on a fire
c A ball or sphere; the earth
d An upward or downward slant
e To shut; to end. Also hot and stuffy
f An exact copy
g A crowd or herd being moved together
h To run away secretly to wed
i Cloud like gases from something burning
j To find it hard to breathe

Six of One; Half a Dozen of the Other

6 The first and last letters are missing from each of the following six-letter words. Each word begins with the same letter and the final letters, when re-arranged, form a word meaning 'fashionable'.

```
— E T H O —
— A R B L —
— O D E S —
— E L O D —
— A S T E —
— A R G I —
```

The jumbled word is _____ .

Word Chain

7 Change MOON to BEAM in four moves by changing one letter at a time to form a new word.

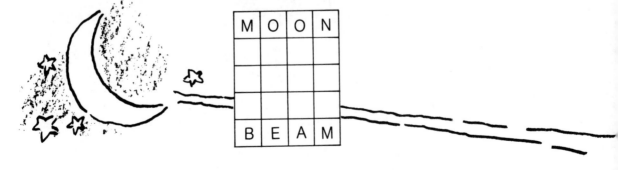

M	O	O	N
B	E	A	M

Unit 4

> decide favourite missile admire
> require surprise practise practice

1 Write each of the list words in your book. Use each one in a sentence of your own.

2 Match the clues with the list words.

   a An action that is repeated many times to gain skill or experience

   b A rocket which can be aimed at a distant object   decide

   c To need; to demand   favourite

   d To repeat a performance many times to gain skill   missile

           admire

   e To make a choice   require

   f Something or someone that is loved above all others   surprise

           practise

   g To have a good opinion of   practice

   h The feeling caused by an unexpected event

Practise or Practice

3 Pract**ice** is a noun, whereas pract**ise** is a verb. Fill the blanks in these sentences with pract**ice** or pract**ise**

   a We have volleyball _____ on Thursday night.

   b Dr Hunter's _____ is on Queen Street.

   c Why don't you _____ what you preach?

   d With _____ he could learn his tables.

   e Tony will _____ the piano every day for one hour.

Find the Word

1	2	3	4	5	6	7	8	9

4 Letters 4, 5, 9, 1 mean wild, uncontrollable anger.
Letters 6, 1, 7, 2 is a tube that carries blood from any part of the body to the heart.
The whole word is a picture printed from an engraved plate.

5 Unjumble the list word in each sentence. Write the sentence in your own book.

a What materials do you (eeuirqr) to complete the job?
b Adonis is so vain he stops to (erimda) himself in front of every mirror.
c Dean couldn't (eicded) which jacket to wear.
d The (upsirrse) party for Lee was difficult to arrange.
e Top tennis players (raptcsie) their skills every day.
f My (vuitfaore) type of ice-cream is chocolate chip.
g The (simlise) hit right on target.
h At football (raticepc) we had to try to kick the ball with our opposite foot.

Crossout

6
a Cross out the colour and find the tree
YEWILLLOLOWW
b Cross out the fruit and find the vegetable
ACAPRBBIACGOTE
c Cross out the bird and find the season
PWARIRNOTTER
d Cross out the city and find the fish
VSAANLCOMUOVNER
e Cross out the country and find the animal
CLLANAADMAA
f Cross out the gem and find the colour
OPUPRAPLLE
g Cross out the insect and find the river
MAOSMQUAIZTOON
h Cross out the sport and find the mountain
HROOCBKSEOYN
i Cross out the season and find the reptile
ACRUTOCUOMNDILE
j Cross out the bird and find the building
SLPIBARARRROYW

Words From People's Names

7 Another **i–e** word is *galvanize*. It means to put a covering of metal, usually zinc, over another metal by using electricity. This process was named after Luigi Galvani, an Italian scientist.

Many of our words come from people's names. It may be their first name, surname, or even their nickname.

Match the words in the box with the people they are associated with. Then find the meaning of each word in a dictionary.

levis	braille	cardigan
nicotine	pavlova	shrapnel

a This food was named after a famous Russian ballerina, Anna Pavlova, after a visit to Australia. The word is _____ and it means _____.

b The seventh Earl of Cardigan (1797–1868), is said to have worn a type of garment that was named after him. The word is _____ and it means _____ .

c The word "jeans" comes from Genoa, a town in Italy where sailors were famous for their cotton pants. But the pants were invented by Levi Strauss, a young immigrant to California. The word is _____ and it means _____ .

d This substance was named after Jean Nicot, a French ambassador to Portugal who introduced tobacco into France about 1560. The word is _____ and it means _____.

e Henry Shrapnel was a British army officer who invented the type of bomb named after him. This bomb explodes into shrapnel. The word is _____ and it means _____.

f This system was named after Louis Braille, a French teacher of the blind who was blind himself after an accident as a young boy. The word is _____ and it means _____.

Unit 5

> costume   produce   include   volume   salute
> furniture   capsule   agriculture   parachute   treasure

1 Write each of the list words in your book. Use each one in a sentence of your own.

2 Fill the blanks in these sentences with list words.

    a Kylie's mother made her a _____ for her part in the school play.
    b The doctor gave Dieter a _____ to swallow.
    c A lot of _____ was burnt when the house caught fire.
    d Emma's father has a stall at the market where he sells groceries and farm _____.
    e The soldiers will _____ the flag to show their respect.
    f In an accident recently a sky-diver died when his _____ didn't open.
    g The divers discovered the pirates' _____ in the sunken ship.
    h What is the _____ of water in the tank?
    i The cost of the trip to Hong Kong did not _____ meals.
    j Better methods of _____ are needed to feed the world's population.

3 Complete this pattern using list words.

More *u–e* Words

4 Here are some more **u–e** words. Find their meanings in a dictionary and write each word with its meaning in your own book.

jute	culture	execute	dune
tribute	altitude	institute	rebuke
crude	attitude	presume	absolute
refute	lure	globule	acute

An 'A' Puzzle

5

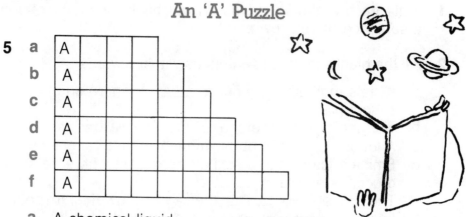

a A chemical liquid
b Watchful and ready. To warn someone
c To help or support
d A female who acts a part in a play or film
e Something unpleasant that happens unexpectedly
f The science that deals with the sun, moon, stars and planets.

Word Quiz

6 How quickly can you find these words?

a A 6-letter word ending in **on**
b A 5-letter word ending in **la**
c A 6-letter word ending in **ol**
d A 7-letter word ending in **ein**
e A 6-letter word ending in **ute**
f A 6-letter word ending in **io**
g A 5-letter word ending in **yl**

Amazing! That took just 10 seconds!

Number Words — Words Meaning Two

7 a Which **du** word means two performers? du __ __

    b Which **bi** word means speaking in two languages? bi __ __ __ __ __ __ __

    c Which **bi** word means every two hundred years? bi __ __ __ __ __ __ __ __ __ __

    d Which **bi** word means an agreement on both sides? bi __ __ __ __ __ __ __

    e Which **bi** word means the muscles of the upper arm? bi __ __ __ __

    f Which **du** word means an exact copy? du __ __ __ __ __ __ __

    g Which **bi** word means twice every year? bi __ __ __ __ __ __

    h Which **bi** word means a plane with two wings? bi __ __ __ __ __

    i Which **du** word means made in two separate parts? du __ __

    j Which **du** word means a fight with deadly weapons between two people? du __ __

    k Which **bi** word is a vehicle with two wheels? bi __ __ __ __ __

    l Which **bi** word means having two wives or husbands at once? bi __ __ __ __

    m Which **bi** word means a woman's swimsuit in two pieces? bi __ __ __ __

    n Which **bi** word means a two-footed animal? bi __ __ __ __

Now use a dictionary to find the meanings of these words.

biannual	bilateral	binoculars	binary
bi-monthly	bifocal	bicultural	bisect

Word Squares

8

V	O	M	I	A
A	Y	S	N	R
G	A	H	T	L
E	C	E	A	E
N	T	L	O	S

List as many words as you can from the letters in the word square. Each word must be made up of letters in squares which touch each other.

Unit 6

ay words

decay payment bayonet dismay portray			
layer prayer array repay essay			

1 Write each of the list words in your book. Use each one in a sentence of your own.

Vertical Words

2 Use the clues to find these seven-letter words. When you have finished, the first column down will give you one of the list words.

a
b
c
d
e
f

a   A person who is being treated by a doctor
b   Getting the meaning of written or printed words. Also the amount shown on the scale of an instrument
c   To consent to or to think well of
d   A language spoken by Jewish people
e   To speak out suddenly in surprise or with strong feeling
f   Let go; let loose or set free

3 Use the clues to complete each word.

a   Money given to settle a debt   __ ay __ __ __ __ __
b   To pay back money that is owed   __ __ __ ay
c   To become rotten or to fall into ruins   __ __ __ ay
d   A flat covering or thickness   __ ay __ __
e   A piece of factual writing, usually short and on one subject   __ __ __ ay
f   To act the part of a character in a play   __ __ __ __ __ __ ay
g   A long knife fixed to the end of a rifle   __ ay __ __ __ __
h   A feeling of fear and hopelessness   __ __ __ __ ay

R You Ready?

4 Add an **R** and rearrange the letters.

a Add **R** to <u>title</u> and get a group of young animals born at the same time to one mother.

b Add **R** to <u>tale</u> and get a word meaning watchful and ready.

c Add **R** to <u>made</u> and get a group of thoughts or images experienced during sleep.

d Add **R** to <u>feat</u> and get at a later time.

e Add **R** to <u>coal</u> and get a song sung at Christmas time. Christmas time.

f Add **R** to <u>heat</u> and get the planet on which we live.

g Add **R** to <u>tidy</u> and get a word meaning not clean.

h Add **R** to <u>tale</u> and get a word meaning to make or become different.

Word Circle

5 Start at the arrow and move around the circle in a clockwise direction. How many words of four letters or more can you find?

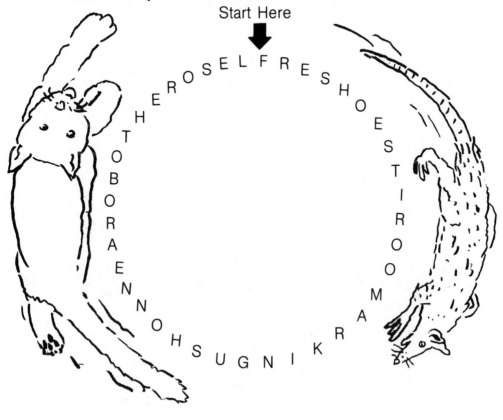

Start Here

THEROSELFRESHOESTIROOMARKINGUSHONNEAROBOT

Add a Letter

6 Follow the directions and put your answers in the boxes below.

a Add one letter to <u>hate</u> to get a word meaning hurry.
b Add one letter to <u>phase</u> to get a group of words.
c Add one letter to <u>cure</u> to get a word meaning to swear.
d Add one letter to <u>paper</u> to get a very poor person.
e Add one letter to <u>write</u> to get a word meaning to twist the body as when in great pain.
f Add one letter to <u>mined</u> to get a word meaning cut into very small pieces.

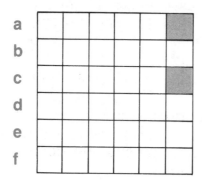

Alphabet Mixture

7 Fill the spaces with letters from the alphabet. Use each letter only once to get eleven words.

A B C D E F G H I J K L M N O P Q R S T U V W X Y Z

_ ET _ CT _ VE
_ UI _ ER
_ U _ IOR
T _ O _ _ ERS
_ UT _ A _
_ ODIA _
_ O _ HURT
_ OSSU _
_ I _ ERN _ TE
_ O _ IC
_ A _ E

Unit 7

y = 'e' words

factor**y** centur**y** especiall**y** naught**y** electricit**y**
enem**y** beaut**y** industr**y** librar**y** secretar**y**

1 Write each of the list words in your book. Use each one in a sentence of your own.

2 Fill the blanks in these sentences with list words.
  a In the last _____ people wore different clothes to what we wear today.
  b The _____ has a new computer.
  c During the strike delivery vans were not able to get goods into the _____.
  d The _____ was advancing towards the city.
  e The large table was made _____ for the dining room.
  f Our _____ supply was cut off when a wild storm brought down the power lines.
  g The most popular book in our _____ is Roald Dahl's *Revolting Rhymes*.
  h The Canadian clothing _____ has a lot of competition from manufacturers in other countries.
  i If you're _____ you won't watch any television.
  j Vancouver is a city of great _____ .

Wear the Champion's Cap

3 Use the letters C, A and P at least once in each row to form seven words.

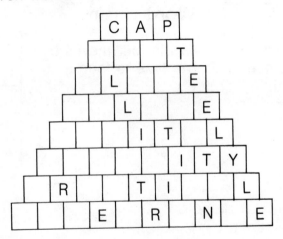

Word Diamonds

4 Use the clues to complete this puzzle.

Across:
2 To break up and move earth
4 Things lit to keep warm
5 A tall broad-leaved tree
Down:
1 Young female people
2 To stop living
3 A precious stone

5 Use the clues to complete each list word.

a A period of 100 years   _ _ _ _ _ _ y
b The power which is produced by friction, by a battery, or by a generator   _ _ _ _ _ _ _ _ _ _ y
c A person with the job of preparing letters, keeping records, arranging meetings, etc.   _ _ _ _ _ _ _ _ y
d A building where goods are made, especially in great quantities by machines   _ _ _ _ _ _ _ y
e A person who hates or dislikes another person   _ _ _ _ y
f To a particularly great degree   _ _ _ _ _ _ _ _ _ y
g The work of factories and large organizations generally   _ _ _ _ _ _ _ y
h Qualities that give pleasure to the senses   _ _ _ _ _ _ y
i Bad in behaviour; not obeying a parent, teacher, set of rules, etc.   _ _ _ _ _ _ _ y
j A building which contains books that may be borrowed by the public   _ _ _ _ _ _ _ y

Word Chain

6 Change FAIL into PASS in four moves by changing one letter at a time to form a new word.

F	A	I	L
P	A	S	S

Anagrams

7 a Change <u>plums</u> into an economic depression.
   b Change <u>lean</u> into a narrow road.
   c Change <u>dances</u> into a word meaning to go up.
   d Change <u>garden</u> into the possibility of harm.
   e Change <u>skater</u> into a thin line or band different from
     what surrounds it.
   f Change <u>runway</u> into not careful; not looking out for
     danger.
   g Change <u>tiredness</u> into people who live in a place and
     are not visitors.
   h Change <u>agrees</u> into a thick oily substance.

Start and Finish

8 Find two letters that will end one word and begin another.
   For example, **ge** is the end of *page* and the start of *gear*.

```
        c i r c ☐ ☐ t t e r
      g e n e r ☐ ☐ p i n e
          b a s ☐ ☐ s e c t
        c h a r i ☐ ☐ t e r
        c i t i z ☐ ☐ o u g h
          t e a ☐ ☐ a r g e
        h e a r ☐ ☐ r o a t
          r o u ☐ ☐ o s t
          k n i ☐ ☐ r r y
          g n o ☐ ☐ t h o d
      r u b b i ☐ ☐ e l f
          v i s i ☐ ☐ i o n
```

9 Which list word when put in this pattern makes 5-letter
   words reading across.

A	B		E	Y
E	R		C	T
B	R		C	E
L	A		G	H
P	A		C	H
L	A		E	R

Here's...

Unit 8

qu words

> question   square   quarry   squash   mosque
> mosquito   equator   quartz   quilt

1 Write each of the list words in your book. Use each one in a sentence of your own.

2 Complete this pattern using list words.

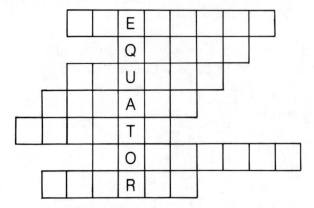

3 Unjumble the list word in each sentence. Write the sentence in your own book.

  a The Anopheles (suimooqt) can carry the disease malaria.
  b They could see the domed roof of the beautiful (omqsue) in the distance.
  c (ztrauQ) is a kind of mineral consisting of silica.
  d Mr Chong asked Pat a (tiqsouen).
  e The stone in that building came from the (rrquay) at Elmdale.
  f The (quotaer) is an imaginary line around the centre of the earth.
  g Saida is making a patchwork (tiqlu) for her bed.
  h Brittany didn't mean to (huassq) Mr Hain's hat.
  i The meeting was held in the village (qusera).

Missing Words

4

> QQQQ OOO M A
> E UUUU III SSSS
> N H TTTT L

Use the letters in this box to make four list words. One letter is left over. Write ten words that begin with the extra letter.

Palindromes

5 Palindromes are words that spell the same whether you go from left to right, or from right to left. Use the clues to find these palindromes. The first one has been done for you.

   a A female sheep EWE

   b Flat, smooth. Also equal in position _ _ _ _ _

   c Twelve o'clock midday _ _ _ _

   d A method of finding the position of a solid object by sending out a pulse of high frequency radio waves

     _ _ _ _ _

   e A narrow covered boat used by the Inuit

     _ _ _ _ _

   f A respectful way of addressing a woman

     _ _ _ _ _

   g The kind of welcome given by the mayor

     _ _ _ _ _

   h Something that makes you conscious or healthy again _ _ _ _ _ _ _

A 'QU' Puzzle

6

a	Q	U			
b	Q	U			
c	Q	U			
d	Q	U			
e	Q	U			
f	Q	U			
g	Q	U			
h	Q	U			

   a A place where boats can load and unload

   b A search, especially for something valuable

   c A creature being hunted. Also a place from which stone is dug out

   d Five people playing or singing together

   e To have an argument

   f A container for arrows. Also to tremble a little

   g To repeat someone else's words in speech or writing

   h A test where questons have to be answered

Word Chains

7 Change COLD to MELT and SEAS to LAND in four moves by changing one letter at a time to form a new word.

C	O	L	D
M	E	L	T

S	E	A	S
L	A	N	D

Cold Words

8 Use the clues to find these words that all contain the letters **ice**

   a   Absence of sound; stillness   __ i __ __ __ ce

   b   Knowledge which can be studied and tested exactly   __ __ i __ __ ce

   c   An addictive chemical in tobacco   __ ic __ __ __ __ __ e

   d   A substance used for treating disease __ __ __ ic __ __ e

   e   A pointed stick which is part of a fence   __ ic __ e __

   f   A repeated performance of a skill (a Unit 4 word) __ __ __ __ __ ice

   g   A two-wheeled vehicle   __ ic __ __ __ e

   h   To cut into very small pieces   __ ice

   i   A living creature that is so small that it cannot be seen without a microscope   __ ic __ __ __ e

   j   Use of bodily force on other people __ i __ __ __ __ ce

Find the Word

9

1	2	3	4	5	6	7	8	9

Letters 6, 1, 2, 4, 8 mean to cut off hair close to the skin with a razor.
Letters 7, 5, 2, 3 mean to pull apart by force.
The whole word means to have cut grain and gathered it in.

Unit 9

history factory calculator scissors interior	
orchestra choral refrigerator radiator monitor	

1 Write each of the list words in your book. Use each one in a sentence of your own.

An 'OR' Puzzle

2

a	O	R			
b		O	R		
c			O	R	
d				O	R
e					O	R
f				O	R
g			O	R	
h		O	R		
i	O	R			

a A songbird that is usually black and orange
b To command not to do something
c Sung by a group or choir
d To send goods out of a country for sale
e A piece of heavy metal for lowering into the water to keep a ship from moving
f To preserve sound or vision so that it can be seen or heard again
g To burn a surface so as to change its colour or taste but without completely destroying it
h A feeling of great shock, fear and dislike
i A starting point

3 Write three list words that can be made from these letters.

L A R T C C O S M O R H I O I S S S R O N

4 Match the list word with the correct definition.

a *Monitor* means
— a pupil chosen by a teacher to help in certain ways
— a kind of instrument for checking the quality of some manufactured goods
— to listen and check on foreign radio broadcasts
— all of the above definitions

b *Choral* means
— a hard substance of various colours found on the bottom of the sea
— an enclosure for horses
— sung by a group or choir
— a number of musical notes

c *Interior* means
— the outside of something; the outer
— the inside of anything; the inner
— the time between two events
— to bring goods into a country from overseas

d A *radiator* is
— the part of a car that holds water to cool the engine
— someone who carries out a surprise attack or raid
— a radioactive metallic element which gives out rays used in treating certain diseases
— a long thin sword used in fencing

e *History* is
— The science that describes the surface of the earth and its inhabitants
— the science that describes the earth's crust, especially the changes in various layers of rocks over millions of years
— the branch of mathematics that deals with bar graphs and histograms
— an account of past events

5 Which list words when put in the spaces make 5-letter words reading across?

L	I		I	T
B	L		O	D
L	I		E	R
I	D		O	T
W	A		E	R
S	T		O	L
B	E		T	H

A	S		E	N
R	A		S	E
V	I		I	T
W	A		C	H
A	M		N	G
P	A		C	H
M	A		O	R

A 'B' Puzzle

6

a | B
b | B
c | B
d | B
e | B
f | B

a The beak of a bird
b Another name for a buffalo
c A small smooth-haired dog used in hunting
d A group of connected electric cells
e A liquid for drinking, especially tea, coffee, etc.
f Things that are built; houses, stores, apartments, etc.

Word Quiz

7 How quickly can you find these words?

a A 6-letter word ending in **ly**
b A 4-letter word ending in **sa**
c A 5-letter word ending in **gh**
d A 4-letter word ending in **ga**
e An 8-letter word ending in **ini**
f A 6-letter word ending in **al**
g A 4-letter word ending in **ol**

Unit 10

Review

1 Choose the correct word.

a	scisors	scissers	scissors
b	monitor	moniter	moneter
c	mosquitoe	mosquito	mosqueto
d	kwestion	queastion	question
e	century	sentury	centery
f	naughty	norty	gnaughty
g	dekay	decaye	decay
h	tresure	treashure	treasure
i	sirprise	surprise	suprise
j	hemisphere	heamisphere	hemisfere
k	parade	parad	perade
l	separate	seperate	seperit
m	langage	languige	language
n	recede	resede	recide
o	mosk	mosgue	mosque

2 Write these words into your own book and group them into *word families*.

strove	choral	enemy
require	quartz	parachute
capsule	radiator	portray
essay	electricity	drone
industry	prayer	climate
secretary	squash	decide
quarry	volume	athlete
calculator	missile	telescope

3 Find the small words that are in the larger words.

chocolate	hemisphere	drone
stampede	strove	surprise
favourite	costume	produce
language	furniture	bayonet
missile	treasure	industry
practice	portray	quartz
replace	factory	squash

Jumbled Words

4 Unjumble each word. Then write the plural for each word.
The first one has been done for you.

a	earpad	parade	parades
b	telateh	_____	_____
c	mehhseripe	_____	_____
d	noze	_____	_____
e	simelis	_____	_____
f	terahpacu	_____	_____
g	yeparr	_____	_____
h	rotcaty	_____	_____
i	yneem	_____	_____
j	toiqsmou	_____	_____
k	rocissss	_____	_____
l	rotalaccul	_____	_____
m	epocselet	_____	_____

Mixed Words

5 Each group of letters contains two words from Units 1 to
9. What are the words?

Example: r e v o k e = revoke

r p e varo a kdee

p ar a d e = parade

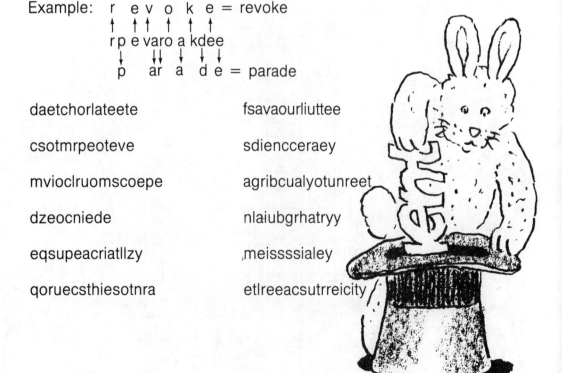

daetchorlateete	fsavaourliuttee
csotmrpeoteve	sdiencceraey
mvioclruomscoepe	agribcualyotunreet
dzeocniede	nlaiubgrhatryy
eqsupeacriatllzy	meissssialey
qoruecsthiesotnra	etlreeacsutrreicity

A Jumbo Word Search

6 How many words from Unit 1 to Unit 9 can you find in this word search? The words go across the page or down the page.

```
I N T E R I O R D R A B
C A R S E D Y E N E M Y
A U N Q P I D F L C F S
R G A U A S D R A E U T
E H D A Y M W I Y D R A
M T M S J A N G E E N M
I Y I H O Y P E R O I P
C H R O M E Q R D S T E
R D E N S Q U A R E U D
O E R A D I A T O R R E
S C E N E F R O N Z E F
C I P N S O R R E L C A
O D L Y F R Y X P I A V
P E A C A L C O R B P O
E A C S C I S S O R S U
Q U E S T I O N D A U R
H I S T O R Y D U R L I
S E P A R A T E C Y E T
D E C A Y A K C E L L E
M O T O R E V O K E C R
Q U I L T P A R A D E I
C O M P E T E A S O L C
A A L M S T O T A P E H
L A N G U A G E L Q B S
C R S A P R O N U A R S
U R I P P E R U T T A I
L A E L O P E T E H T N
A Y E S S A Y S R L E C
T T E L E S C O P E S E
O R C H E S T R A T U R
R U H E M I S P H E R E
Z M O N I T O R C O P E
O E R I W A S T E R R D
N R A M I S S I L E I I
E E L P S T R O V E S N
C O M P L E T E W E E E
```

Unit 11

er words

messenger whether deserve passenger shoulder saucer exercise different dangerous government

1 Write each of the list words in your book. Use each one in a sentence of your own.

Which Word To Use?

2 Fill the blank in each sentence with the correct form of the list word.

  a He _____ the award for his acts of bravery.
     (deserve, deserves, deservedly, deserving)
  b The doctor _____ his way through the crowd.
     (shoulder shoulders, shouldered, shouldering)
  c When Robina was training for the gymnastics competition she _____ for two hours every day.
     (exercise, exercises, exercising, exercised)
  d My older brother doesn't know the _____ between asking and demanding.
     (differ, difference, different, differential)
  e It's _____ to skate on thin ice.
     (danger, dangers, dangerous, dangerously)
  f Elected members of parliament _____ Canada.
     (govern, government, governor, governable)

Correct Endings

3 Place **ary, ory, ury** or **ery** into the correct spaces.

Febru _ _ _	ordin _ _ _	cent _ _ _
fact _ _ _	diction _ _ _	monast _ _ _
hist _ _ _	Janu _ _ _	sal _ _ _
libr _ _ _	mis _ _ _	vict _ _ _
can _ _ _	bound _ _ _	fi _ _ _
lux _ _ _	mem _ _ _	slipp _ _ _
groc _ _ _	deliv _ _ _	mission _ _ _
discov _ _ _	myst _ _ _	necess _ _ _

Boxed Words

4 Two list words are jumbled up in each of the boxes below. What are the words? To help you, the <u>first</u> letter of one word and the <u>last</u> letter of the other word are circled.

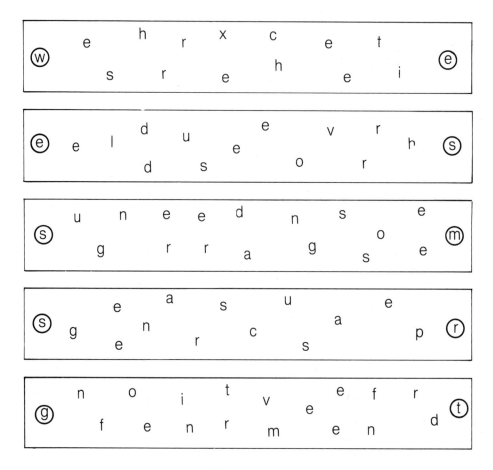

Anagrams

5 **a** Change <u>cares</u> into a word meaning to cause sudden fear.
  b Change <u>mugs</u> into a word meaning self-satisfied.
  c Change <u>master</u> into a natural flow of water, usually smaller than a river.
  d Change <u>reveals</u> into a word meaning more than two but fewer than many.
  e Change <u>eastern</u> into a word meaning the closest.
  f Change <u>leapt</u> into part of a flower.
  g Change <u>ocean</u> into a small boat moved by a paddle.
  h Change <u>rental</u> into a horn of a deer.

6 Which list words when put in the spaces make 5-letter words reading across?

A	D		I	T
C	L		A	R
B	A		I	N
E	A		E	L
A	L		R	T
B	A		J	O
N	I		H	T
F	I		L	D
D	I		T	Y

D	O		G	E
C	L		S	H
F	I		A	L
L	I		H	T
S	H		E	P
F	O		G	E
A	B		V	E
F	L		T	E
W	A		P	S

T	O		I	C
B	E		C	H
W	A		T	E
V	I		I	T
C	L		R	K
B	I		G	O
F	I		H	T
D	R		A	M
F	O		C	E

B	A		G	E
A	G		L	E
O	F		E	R
G	I		T	S
S	H		E	T
F	O		T	H
T	R		A	T
D	E		S	E
A	C		O	R

Top of the Class!

7 Use the letters T, O, and P at least once in each row to form six words.

Unit 12

More *er* words

daughter	consider	minister	drawer	laughter
prisoner	recover	dessert	lantern	

1 Write each of the list words in your book. Use each one in a sentence of your own.

2 Unjumble the list word in each sentence.

   a The elderly woman kept her money hidden in the bottom (radrew) of her wardrobe.

   b The (rughlaet) of the children could be heard around the school ground.

   c Does the price of the meal include (tressed)?

   d Queen Elizabeth II was the (rehguadt) of King George VI.

   e We took a gas (tenlarn) with us when we went camping.

   f I (disconer) Monica Hughes' latest book the best one she has ever written.

   g The (pioersnr) was locked away in the Tower of London.

   h The army was unable to (cerevor) any of the territory it had lost.

   i Kim Campbell was Canada's first female Prime (tniMiesr).

Word Chain

3 Change ROSE to PINK in four moves by changing one letter at a time to form a new word.

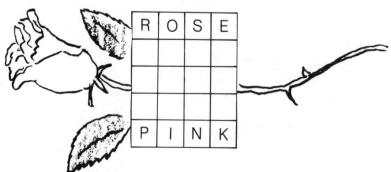

R You Ready?

4 Add **R** and rearrange the letters.

  a Add **R** to <u>coat</u> and get a person who acts in a film or play.
  b Add **R** to <u>stub</u> and get a word meaning to break open suddenly.
  c Add **R** to <u>teen</u> and get a word meaning to come into a place.
  d Add **R** to <u>mace</u> and get the rich fatty part of milk.
  e Add **R** to <u>even</u> and get a small thread-like part of your body that carries messages to and from the brain.
  f Add **R** to <u>teem</u> and get an instrument for measuring a quantity of something, such as gas, water or electricity.
  g Add **R** to <u>dole</u> and get a word meaning having lived longer than someone else.
  h Add **R** to <u>kind</u> and get a word meaning to swallow water, milk, or some other liquid.
  i Add **R** to <u>page</u> and get a green or purple fruit that grows in bunches on a vine.
  j Add **R** to <u>shoe</u> and get an animal used for riding or pulling carts.

Vertical Words

5 Use the clues to find these 7-letter words. When you have finished, the first column down will give you one of the list words.

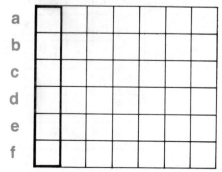

  a A sea mammal like a porpoise but with a slender, pointed snout
  b To move or turn in the opposite direction
  c A statement of money received and paid with a balance
  d A shrill sound made by forcing breath through the lips
  e Graceful; refined
  f Another word for umpire

36

Crossout

6 **a** Cross out the animal and find the country
L S C E O O T P L A A R N D D

b Cross out the sport and find the season
T S P E R N N I N I G S

c Cross out the planet and find the subject
J M U P A T H I E M T A T I E C R S

d Cross out the month and find the fruit
A C H U E G R U R S T Y

e Cross out the vegetable and find the city
P P A U M R P I K S I N

f Cross out the river and find the insect
N B U I T T E L R F E L Y

g Cross out the sport and find the part of the body
R S T U O G M B A C Y H

h Cross out the disaster and find the vehicle
H T U R R I A C I A N N E

i Cross out the flower and find the month
V O I C O T O L B E E T R

j Cross out the jewel and find the animal
D M I O A N M K O N E D Y

Break the Code

7 In this code the letter 'a' is 2A, 'f' is 5B, and so on. Use the code to find these list words.

	1	2	3	4	5
A	e	a	g	t	n
B	l	r	b	x	f
C	m	c	u	q	o
D	d	j	y	h	p
E	k	w	v	i	s

a 2C, 5C, 5A, 5E, 4E, 1D, 1A, 2B
b IC, 4E, 5A, 4E, 5E, 4A, 1A, 2B
c 1B, 2A, 5A, 4A, 1A, 2B, 5A
d 1D, 2B, 2A, 2E, 1A, 2B
e 5D, 2B, 4E, 5E, 5C, 5A, 1A, 2B

Unit 13

wh words

whistle   whisper   whether
wharf   whine   whisker   whimper

1 Write each of the list words in your book. Use each one in a sentence of your own.

2 Fill the blanks in these sentences with list words.

a The boats unloaded their cargo at the _____.
b When the boy was punished he began to _____.
c The dog began to _____ because he was alone.
d I heard the wind _____ through the trees.
e Ahmed won the race by a _____ .
f Julian didn't know _____ to read a book or play on the computer.
g Lise-Anne couldn't _____ after she lost her front tooth.

Jumbled Words

3 Rearrange the letters to form list words

hhewetr   niwhe
kisherw   hwmirep
hstwiel   sewrphi
fawhr

More *wh* Words

4 Find the meanings of these **wh** words in your dictionary and use them in sentences.

wheeze   whet   whim
whimsical   whirl   whisk
whittle   whorl   wholesome

5 Match the list word with the correct definition.

a A *wharf* is
— either of two equal parts into which something is divided
— a wild animal of the dog family which hunts in a pack
— a word meaning to eat quickly in large amounts
— a platform built into the sea where ships load and unload goods

b *Whine* means
— to complain in an irritating way
— to make a high sad sound
— an alcoholic drink made from grapes or other fruit, plants, etc.
— a loud shout of joy

c A *whisker* is
— one of the long, stiff hairs near the mouth of a cat, mouse, etc.
— a small hand-held apparatus for beating eggs, whipping cream, etc.
— a strong alcoholic drink made from grain
— a type of edible sea fish

d *Whimper* means
— to make a small, weak cry
— a gentle sound made by a horse
— to move round and round very fast
— to remove water from clothes by twisting

e *Whether* means
— the condition of wind, rain, sunshine, snow, etc. at a certain time
— to pass safely through a storm
— a type of fat lamb raised for its meat
— if, or, no matter if

I think I smell a rat

A 'V' Puzzle

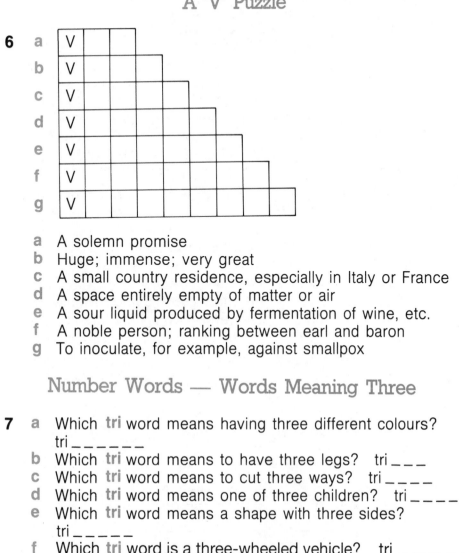

6

a A solemn promise
b Huge; immense; very great
c A small country residence, especially in Italy or France
d A space entirely empty of matter or air
e A sour liquid produced by fermentation of wine, etc.
f A noble person; ranking between earl and baron
g To inoculate, for example, against smallpox

Number Words — Words Meaning Three

7
a Which **tri** word means having three different colours?
tri _ _ _ _ _ _
b Which **tri** word means to have three legs?   tri _ _ _
c Which **tri** word means to cut three ways?   tri _ _ _ _
d Which **tri** word means one of three children?   tri _ _ _ _
e Which **tri** word means a shape with three sides?
tri _ _ _ _ _
f Which **tri** word is a three-wheeled vehicle?   tri _ _ _ _ _
g Which **tri** word is the provincial flower of Ontario?
tri _ _ _ _ _
h Which **tri** word means occurring every three years?
tri _ _ _ _ _ _
i Which **tri** word is a boat with three hulls side by side?
tri _ _ _ _ _
j Which **tri** word means a group of three performers?   tri _
k Which **tri** word means three children born at the same
time to the one mother?   tri _ _ _ _ _

8   Find the meaning of these words in the dictionary.

trilogy   trillion
trinity   triple
triplicate   trimester
trivet   triceps

Unit 14

ch words

handker**ch**ief sandwi**ch** **ch**ocolate **ch**aracter **ch**oir
ma**ch**ine stoma**ch** **ch**emical **ch**ose **ch**imney

1 Write each of the list words in your book. Use each one in
a sentence of your own.

Triangle Words

2 In the outer triangle you will find the first letter of each of
three list words. In the next triangle, moving towards the
centre, is the second letter, and so on. What are the
words?

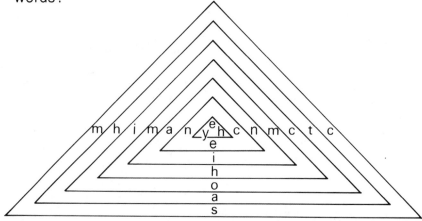

More *ch* Words

3 Here are some more **ch** words. Find their meanings in a
dictionary and write each word with its meaning in your
own book.

chafe	chaise	poach
lynch	exchequer	chaos
machete	chaff	lurch
chalet	chameleon	fuchsia
chauffeur	chasm	chisel

4 Fill the blanks in these sentences with list words.

   a Jamal had a banana _____ for lunch.
   b Acid is a dangerous _____ that can burn.
   c After the strong wind storm we had to repair the
     _____ .
   d The defeated candidate _____ not to run for
     Parliament again.
   e The school _____ sang beautifully at the concert.
   f Ophelia is the main female _____ in the play *Hamlet*.
   g The washing _____ needs repairing.
   h The boxer did a lot of exercises to strengthen his
     _____ before the title fight.
   i The museum had an interesting display which included
     a beautiful lace _____ once owned by Queen Victoria.
   j Peter likes milk _____ but I prefer dark _____.

Words From People's Names

5 Match the words in the box with the people they are
associated with. Then find the meaning of each word in a
dictionary.

guillotine	diesel	bloomers
bobby	dahlia	pasteurisation

   a This garment was named after an American woman,
Amelia J. Bloomer (1818–94), who advocated this type
of clothing in a magazine she published. She was
regarded as a social reformer. The word is _____ and
it means _____.
   b This flower was named after Anders Dahl (1751–89), a
Swedish botanist. The word is _____ and it means
_____.
   c Rudolf Diesel (1858–1913),a German engineer who
invented the diesel engine in the 1890's, is responsible
for this word being a part of our language. The word is
_____ and it means _____.
   d This machine was named after Joseph Guillotin
(1738–1814), a French doctor who suggested using it
for executing people by cutting off their heads. The
word is _____ and it means _____.

e This title was named after Sir Robert Peel who began the London police force. The word is _____ and it means _____.

f Louis Pasteur (1822–95), the French scientist who invented the process of heating milk to destroy bacteria, had this process named after him. The word is _____ and it means _____.

6 Use the clues to complete each word.

a A group of people trained to sing together
ch__ __ __

b A substance used in chemistry   ch __ __ __ __ __ __

c Square of linen, cotton, silk, etc. used to wipe the nose   __ __ __ __ __ __ __ ch__ __ __

d An instrument, usually made of metal, designed to do a particular job   __ __ ch __ __ __

e A sweet brown food or drink made from cocoa
ch__ __ __ __ __ __ __

f A structure designed to carry away smoke   ch__ __ __ __ __ __

g To have made a choice   ch__ __ __

h What a person is like, for example, honest or nasty   ch__ __ __ __ __ __ __ __

i A part of your body which holds food after it has been swallowed   __ __ __ __ __ __ ch

j Two pieces of bread with meat or some other food between them   __ __ __ __ __ __ __ ch

7 Arrange the following groups of ch words into alphabetical order.

a chemical   christen   character   chord
b technical   echo   stomach   ache
c headache   chorus   school   scholar
d choir   Christmas   chimney   chose
e machine   sandwich   chocolate   chemical
f lynch   lurch   chaos   poach

Unit 15

ss words

gue**ss** succe**ss** sci**ss**ors busine**ss** nece**ss**ary address blo**ss**om po**ss**ible me**ss**age ma**ss**age

1 Write each of the list words in your book. Use each one in a sentence of your own.

2 Fill the blanks in these sentences with list words.

   a If you're out in the snow for a long time you should
      _____ your cheeks so that they won't get frostbitten.
   b Take whatever tools are _____ to get the job done.
   c I received a _____ that she would be late.
   d There were two _____ solutions to the puzzle.
   e The school concert was a great _____.
   f Colin is left-handed and finds it difficult to cut with
      most _____.
   g You win a prize if you can _____ how many jelly
      beans are in the jar.
   h My uncle owns a small _____ in Red Deer.
   i Orange _____ has a lovely scent.
   j On the form I had to print my name and _____.

3 Fill each blank with either **s** or **ss**

heire __	succe __	po __ um	ver __ e
trespa __	u __ eful	trou __ ers	gra __ p
famou __	worthle __	ve __ el	dre __ maker
wilderne __	expre __	usele __	di __ may
pa __ age	witne __	ta __ el	di __ mi __
mi __ er	mi __ take	a __ ist	a __ cend

Word Square

4 List as many words as you can from the letters in the word square. Each word must be made up of letters in squares which touch each other.

B	E	T	N
A	L	L	E
Y	R	T	V
C	A	E	M

Word Chains

5 Change BEAR into TRAP and RIDE into MULE in four moves by changing one letter at a time to form a new word.

B	E	A	R
T	R	A	P

R	I	D	E
M	U	L	E

6 Use the clues to complete each word.

  a   A tool with two sharp edges used for cutting cloth and paper _ _ _ ss _ _ _

  b   Information sent from one person to another _ _ ss _ _ _

  c   To state an opinion without knowing for sure _ _ _ ss

  d   The place where one lives _ _ _ _ _ ss

  e   Something that cannot be done without _ _ _ _ ss _ _ _

  f   Rubbing and manipulating parts of the body to make them stronger or to relieve pain _ _ ss _ _ _

  g   The flower on a tree which comes before the fruit _ _ _ ss _ _

  h   A satisfactory ending to something you set out to do _ _ _ _ _ ss

  i   Occupation; work _ _ _ _ _ _ _ ss

  j   Able to be done _ _ ss _ _ _ _

Six of One; Half a Dozen of the Other

7 The first and last letters are missing from each of the following six-letter words. Each word begins with the same letter, and the final letters, when rearranged, form a word meaning the part of an object which you hold onto.

_ C A R E _
_ A D D L _
_ A N D A _
_ C O R C _
_ E A S O _
_ I E S T _

The jumbled word is _____.

Anagrams

8 **a** Change <u>cedars</u> into a word meaning frightened.
   b Change <u>ascot</u> into the land next to the sea.
   c Change <u>bared</u> into hair on the face below the mouth.
   d Change <u>sedate</u> into having unkindly made fun of.
   e Change <u>resin</u> into a word meaning to wash with water.
   f Change <u>thus</u> into small buildings often made of wood.
   g Change <u>ether</u> into a number.
   h Change <u>relace</u> into a breakfast food which is made from grain.

'A' Words

9

a	A						
b		A					
c			A				
d			A				
e				A			
f					A		
g						A	
h					A		
i				A			
j			A				
k			A				
l		A					
m	A						

a To go away forever from something or someone; to leave behind
b A building where things are made in large quantities, usually by machines
c Part of the wing or the soft coat of a bird
d A man whose task is to kill a bull in a bullfight
e A piece of cloth for covering up a wound
f In place of
g A food flavouring — often used in ice-cream
h A type of car or a famous Ottawa Indian chief
i Information sent from one person to another
j To take air into the body and force it out again
k Swinging or moving from side to side
l Something put up to prevent anyone passing
m The lower part of the body which contains the stomach

Unit 16

Silent Letters

| g**u**ard   g**u**ide   s**c**ience   s**c**ene |
| c**h**emistry   stoma**ch**   hym**n**   colum**n** |

1 Write each of the list words in your book. Use each one in a sentence of your own.

2 Fill the blank in each sentence with the correct form of the list word.

   a Three soldiers _____ the prince whenever he left the palace.
      (g**u**ard, g**u**ards, g**u**arded, g**u**arding)

   b The climbers needed someone to _____ them to the mountain.
      (g**u**ide, misg**u**ide, g**u**ides, g**u**ided, g**u**idance)

   c Marta is hopeless at French but she is very good in _____ .
      (s**c**ience, s**c**iences, s**c**ientific, s**c**ientifically)

   d The _____ on the mountain is breathtaking.
      (s**c**ene, s**c**enes, s**c**enery, s**c**enic)

   e For his birthday, Sean was given a _____ set.
      (c**h**emist, c**h**emists, c**h**emistry, c**h**emical)

   f The _____ wrote a very critical article about the Prime Minister.
      (colum**n**, colum**n**s, colum**n**ar, colum**n**ist)

Different Meanings

3 Each of these three sentences has a different meaning of the word *column*. Write each sentence in your own book and next to it write the meaning of the word <u>column</u>.

   a The account of the bank robbery filled nearly a <u>column</u>.
   b The roof of the Town Hall was supported by eight <u>columns</u>.
   c Evelyn had to add up a <u>column</u> of figures.

4 Match the list word with the definition.

a The place where a thing happened — guard

b The part of the body in which food is digested — guide

c The scientific study of what substances are made of — science

d To keep safe or defend from danger — scene

e A song of praise in a church service — chemistry

f To show someone the way — stomach

g A set of figures arranged above each other — hymn

h Knowledge of facts gained through study and experiment — column

5 Which list words when put in the spaces make 5-letter words reading across?

W	A		T	E
F	O		U	S
Y	I		L	D
H	O		E	Y
W	R		C	K

A	R		U	E
Y	O		N	G
H	E		V	E
F	I		S	T
O	L		E	R

Jumbled Words

6 Rearrange the letters to form list words.

a daugr   c lmuocn   e censice   g tomsahc

b ysiechmtr d diuge   f myhn   h enecs

ence or *ance*

7 The list word *science* ends in **ence** Complete these words using either **ence** or **ance**

pati _ _ _ _   sent _ _ _ _   appear _ _ _ _

sci _ _ _ _   bal _ _ _ _   interfer _ _ _ _

perform _ _ _ _   insur _ _ _ _   entr _ _ _ _

influ _ _ _ _   experi _ _ _ _   ambul _ _ _ _

sil _ _ _ _   nuis _ _ _ _   refer _ _ _ _

differ _ _ _ _   independ _ _ _ _   dist _ _ _ _

guid _ _ _ _   accept _ _ _ _   differ _ _ _ _

Word Quiz

8 How quickly can you find these words?

    a A 6-letter word ending in **sue**
    b A 5-letter word ending in **ue**
    c A 5-letter word ending in **cht**
    d A 7-letter word ending in **kle**
    e A 4-letter word ending in **ey**
    f A 7-letter word ending in **oon**
    g A 5-letter word ending in **um**

N-dings

9 Use the clues to find these 7-letter words that all end in **N**

a A						N
b B						N
c C						N
d D						N
e E						N
f F						N
g G						N
h H						N
i K						N
j L						N

    a A pain-killing medicine, usually in white tablets
    b Something you buy that costs less than the usual price
    c A soft pillow covered with pretty material. Often used to rest against on a chair or couch
    d A container into which you sweep dust
    e To give the meaning of something; to make it clear
    f A book about people and events that are not really true
    g A large sailing ship which was used by the Spaniards hundreds of years ago
    h The place where the earth and sky appear to meet
    i A room where cooking is done
    j A metal and glass container for a candle or oil light

Unit 17

Soft 'g' words

danger	imagine	college	general	pigeon
revenge	marriage	genius	manager	lounge

1 Write each of the list words in your book. Use each one in a sentence of your own.

2 Fill the blank in each sentence with the correct form of the list word.

   a It is _____ to skate on thin ice.
   (danger, dangers, dangerous, dangerously)
   b All the characters in the book are _____.
   (imagine, imaginary, imagination, imaginative)
   c The painter developed his style while still at art _____.
   (college, collegial, collegian, collegiate)
   d Women, _____ speaking, live longer than men.
   (general, generality, generally, generalise)
   e He sought _____ for the harm they had done him.
   (revenge, revenged, revengeful, revenging)
   f The minister has _____ over 200 couples.
   (marry, married, marriage, marriageable)
   g Mr Singh has a new job _____ a chain of supermarkets.
   (manage, manager, managing, management)
   h Robyn was _____ around in front of the t.v.
   (lounge, lounged, lounger, lounging)

3 Write three list words that can be made from these letters:

   G E M I N I M A N O E P I N R A E A G G

Boxed Words

4 Two list words are jumbled up in each of the boxes below. What are the words? To help you, the <u>first</u> letter of one word and the <u>last</u> letter of the other word are circled.

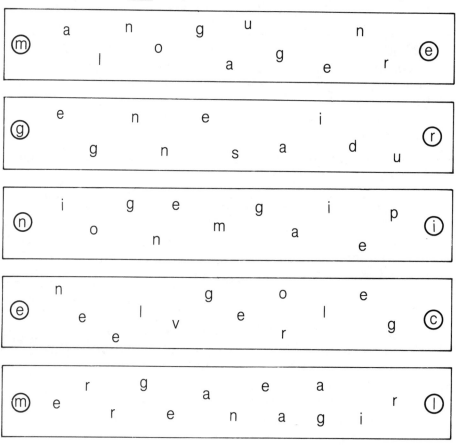

Start and Finish

5 Find two letters that will end one word and begin another.

```
    N E E D □ □ A G U E
    I G U A □ □ V I G A T O R
P R E C I O □ □ U A L
    S Q U A □ □ D U C E
  M E S S A □ □ Y S E R
F O O T S T □ □ I S O D E
    E N O U □ □ A S T L Y
    D R A G □ □ W A R D S
O P E R A T □ □ I G I N A L
    C R U S A □ □ L I V E R
```

Vertical Words

6 Use the clues to find these seven-letter words. When you have finished, the first column down will give you a list word.

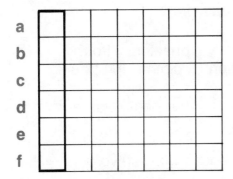

a A movable lock, turned by a key, for fastening gates, etc.
b A huge mass of ice floating in the sea
c A soldier of very high rank
d When the moon comes between the earth and the sun and partly hides the sun from us for a time
e The largest of all birds. It runs fast but does not fly
f Not taking one side or the other in a dispute, especially a war

Target Words

7 In the outer circle you will find the first letters of five list words. As you move towards the centre you will find the second letter, then the third, and so on. What are the words?

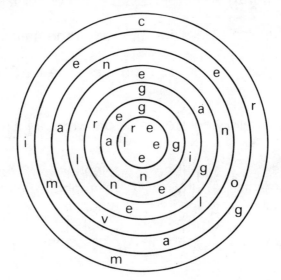

Unit 18

phrase	physical	pharmacy	phantom	trophy
microphone	sphere	graph	dolphin	prophet

1 Write each of the list words in your book. Use each one in a sentence of your own.

2 Fill the blanks in these sentences with list words.

    a As soon as Karen left school she was able to get a job as a clerk in the _____ .

    b Had he actually seen his long-lost brother or was it only a _____?

    c Yesterday in class we drew a _____ to show the months of our birthdays.

    d Because the sailor could predict storms several days in advance, he was considered by some to be a _____ .

    e Even though the Prime Minister was speaking through a _____ , the noise of the demonstrators drowned her out.

    f A globe is a _____ .

    g After his heart attack, Mr Morris had to do mild _____ exercise each day.

    h In the words of the old _____ 'It's better late than never'.

    i At Marineland we were amazed at the antics of the _____.

    j The winning golfer received a cheque for $10,000 and a silver _____ .

3 Arrange the following groups of **ph** words in alphabetical order.

a	phrase	alphabet	telephone	telegraph
b	photograph	trophy	microphone	sphere
c	physical	graph	elephant	dolphin
d	geography	orphan	prophet	triumph
e	nephew	cellophane	catastrophe	pharmacy
f	phantom	graph	pheasant	physique

4 Match the list word with the correct definition.

a A *phrase* is
— a stage of development
— changes in the appearance of the moon
— a small group of words
— a small flute that plays high notes

b *Physical* means
— feeling ill with a high temperature
— concerning the body
— a person who studies physics
— another word for doctor

c A *dolphin* is
— the son of a king
— a salt-water mammal related to the whale
— a depressing mood
— a fan for a child's toy

d A *sphere* is
— a round figure in space
— a ball-shaped mass
— an area of force or action
— all of the above

e A *phantom* is
— something that appears to be real but isn't
— a type of soft drink
— an elephant driver in Burma
— the ruler of ancient Egypt

f A *graph* is
— a painful swollen lump on the side of the throat
— a piece of healthy skin or bone used to replace a damaged part of the body
— a type of mineral from a meteorite
— a drawing showing the relationship between two things (variables)

Ring Words

5 Look at the letters below and see if you can find the 9-letter word hiding there. Start anywhere, but use each letter once only and move along the lines connecting the circles.

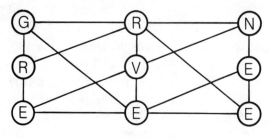

A 'U' Puzzle

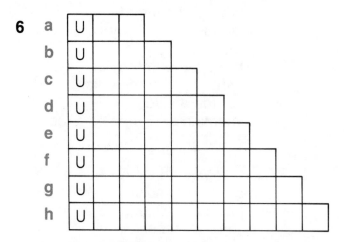

6

a A vase in which the ashes of a dead person are kept
b Unpleasant to see
c To join together into one
d A judge in charge of a game such as baseball
e An imaginary horse-like animal with one horn
f An arrangement of cloth over a frame, used for keeping rain off the head
g The clothes worn next to the body under other clothes
h A place of education at the highest level

Word Puzzle

7 How many words of four letters or more can you make from the letters in the box? Each word must contain the large letter, and each letter can be used only once in each word.

K	I	T
	N	E
D	L	E

Unit 19

ie words

1 Write each of the list words in your book. Use each one in a sentence of your own.

Jumbled Words

2 Rearrange the letters to form list words.

chiaeev   firge
caehhkrindfe   prei
rikseh   lehsid
eeeiblv   ceine
eicep   feiler

3 Fill the blanks in these sentences with list words

    a Is it possible to _____ perfection in any sport?
    b Marika took her _____ to the live performance of *Secret Garden*.
    c The ship's cook prepared a _____ of salt pork.
    d We heard the piercing _____ of the train's whistle as it approached the crossing.
    e Mai wiped her eyes with her _____ .
    f The sword glanced off the knight's _____ .
    g I do not _____ in ghosts.
    h Cameron and Brent went fishing from the end of the _____ .
    i For _____ of your headache, try relaxing in a hot bath.
    j No one could help him in his time of _____ .

Missing Words

4 Can you find four list words that have gone missing and are hiding in the circle?

i r
g e s
h r e i p r
i f e l i l
f e e d

56

Word Quiz

5 How quickly can you find these words?

a A 9-letter word ending in **lia**
b A 5-letter word ending in **pt**
c A 6-letter word ending in **ire**
d A 5-letter word ending in **wel**
e A 4-letter word ending in **em**
f An 8-letter word ending in **lla**
g A 4-letter word ending in **pe**

R You Ready?

6 Add an **R** and rearrange the letters.

a Add R to pod and get a tiny bead of water.
b Add R to mud and get a hollow instrument that you beat to make music.
c Add R to yale and get a word meaning in good time, or near the beginning.
d Add R to mice and get something wrong that can be punished by law.
e Add R to lane and get a word meaning to find out about things or how to do something.
f Add R to age and get the working part of a car or bicycle which changes the speed.
g Add R to bade and get the hair on a man's chin.
h Add R to ail and get someone who tells lies.
i Add R to gale and get a word meaning very big.
j Add R to pig and get a word meaning to hold onto something tightly.

Capital Cities

7 Make sure you know how to spell Canada's capital cities. They are:

Ottawa
St. John's
Halifax
Charlottetown
Fredericton

Quebec
Toronto
Winnipeg
Regina

Edmonton
Victoria
Yellowknife
Whitehorse

Does It Make Sense?

8 Circle all the groups of letters below that would make a
word if **ie** was placed in the blanks.

toff __ __   gr __ __ f   fr __ __ ze   ch __ __ f
br __ __ f   fl __ __ t   rec __ __ ve   g __ __ r
eer __ __   h __ __ ght   r __ __ gn   pat __ __ nce
ch __ __ se   sh __ __ ld   bel __ __ ve   proc __ __ d
shr __ __ k   s __ __ ge   rel __ __ ve   r __ __ ndeer
p __ __ ce   n __ __ ce   s __ __ ze   terr __ __ r

Word Diamonds

9 Use the clues to complete these puzzles.

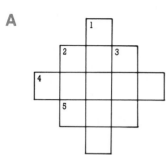

A

B

Across:
2 To ask for food or money
4 A book of fiction
5 Opposite of dry

Down:
1 Equal in position or standard
2 To bend the head forward
   to show respect
3 To receive or obtain

Across:
2 To express in words
4 A small copy
5 To prohibit

Down:
1 A term of respect
   used in addressing
   a woman
2 To cry softly
3 A Japanese coin

Word Chain

10 Here's a word chain with a real
challenge. Change SICK to WELL in
seven moves by changing one letter at a
time to form a new word.

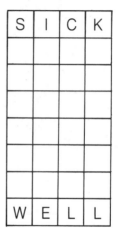

Unit 20

Review

1 Choose the correct word.

a	passengor	passanger	passenger
b	dangerous	dangerus	danjerous
c	sorcer	saucer	saucor
d	goverment	government	govnerment
e	lafter	laughtor	laughter
f	wissel	whistle	whisel
g	handkerchief	handkercheif	handcerkief
h	sandwich	sandwhich	sandwitch
i	charactor	character	charractor
j	sucess	succes	success
k	hym	himn	hymn
l	stomache	stomach	stomick
m	pidgeon	pigeon	pidgon
n	graph	graphe	graff
o	pharmacy	pharmercy	farmacy
p	niece	neice	neece

2 Write these words into your book and group them into *word families*.

believe	phrase	sphere
college	science	massage
business	chemistry	whimper
choir	minister	dessert
exercise	whether	machine
possible	dolphin	guard
grief	lantern	genius
manager	wharf	guess
deserve	column	chocolate

3 Find the small words that are in the larger words.

messenger	deserve	drawer
whisper	handkerchief	business
sandwich	passenger	chocolate
pharmacy	revenge	danger
piece	shoulder	pigeon

Jumbled Words

4 Unjumble each word. Then write the plural for each word. The first has been done for you.

a	gipoen	pigeon	pigeons
b	gnarmae	_____	_____
c	hcyparam	_____	_____
d	cinee	_____	_____
e	nrtnale	_____	_____
f	wkseihr	_____	_____
g	rthyop	_____	_____
h	hnsacidw	_____	_____
i	cossssir	_____	_____
j	seihld	_____	_____
k	hparg	_____	_____
l	sunegi	_____	_____
m	cuasre	_____	_____

Mixed Words

5 Each group of letters contains two words from Units 11 to 19. What are the words?

Example:
```
p     r o p h e t   = prophet
↑     ↑↑ ↑ ↑ ↑ ↑
p m a r o s p s h a e g t e
↓ ↓   ↓   ↓   ↓   ↓   ↓
m a   s   s   a   g   e   = massage
```

awddhriensse   groevceornmvenert
pcrihsoosneer   cwhheemithestrry
mbelossssaogme   wghuiistdlee
mgircrioephfone   ipmhagaintnoem
smacrreiangee   chharyactmern
sdihfrfieereknt   neccehssoariyr

A Jumbo Word Search

8 How many words from Unit 11 to Unit 19 can you find in this word search? The words go across the page and down the page.

```
M M O G C S P W H I N E
M I C R O P H O N E N D
H N H A N H Y S H Y M N
A I E P S E S H I E L D
N S M H I R I O P C G A
D T I A D E C U I H U U
K E S Y E T A L E O I G
E R T U R E L D R I D H
R E L I E F S E D R E T
C X D I F F E R E N T E
H E A Y L A U G H T E R
I R P R I S O N E R L W
E C B L O S S O M W A H
F I W H I S P E R I N I
E S D A N G E R d M T S
N E P T R O P H Y A E K
G U A R D E S D A G R Y
Y M S A U C E R T I N B
D E S E R V E H S N U U
R S E S D A Y G U E S S
F S N C H O S E C R I I
D E G A Y P I E C E S N
A N E T A D D R E S S E
D G R U S C I S S O R S
R E C O V E R R S D A S
A R G O V E R N M E N T
W H I S T L E Y S U N D
E W D T A O W H A R F A
R H C O L U M N R C N N
E I Y M T N O Y E H I E
C M E A S G T E V O E E
D P S C I E N C E O C R
V E C H R M A N N S E O
E R E A M A N A G E R U
R U N R D E S S E R T S
W H E T H E R G R I E F
```

Unit 21

| possible   whistle   bicycle   terrible   probable |
| responsible   muscle   eagle   cable   article |

---

1 Write each of the list words in your book. Use each one in a sentence of your own.

2 Match the clues with the list words.

    a A two-wheeled vehicle

    b The fleshy parts of the body that help us move

    c A very strong, thick rope sometimes made from wire

    d Able to be done

    e Dreadful; awful

    f A large bird of prey with a sharp curved beak and claws

    g To make a sound by blowing through your mouth

    h A piece written in a newspaper or magazine

    i Looking after someone or something

    j Likely to happen

possible
whistle
bicycle
terrible
probable
responsible
muscle
eagle
cable
article

Possible and *Probable*

3 A thing is **possible** if it can happen or is able to be done; and **probable** if it is likely to happen.
For example:
The weather report says rain is **possible** — it can happen.
The weather report says rain is **probable** — it is likely to happen.

4

Which list words when put in the spaces make 5-letter words reading across?

B	E		R	D
E	R		O	R
M	O		T	O
C	H		N	A
Y	A		H	T
V	A		U	E
C	H		S	S

A	B		O	T
C	H		R	P
O	C		U	R
L	O		A	L
U	N		L	E
S	I		L	Y
E	V		R	Y

V	O		E	L
A	S		E	N
C	H		M	E
N	A		T	Y
O	T		E	R
T	U		I	P
E	R		C	T

5

Fill the blanks in these sentences with list words.

a Who is _____ for this mess?

b There is only one _____ solution to that problem.

c The weather forecast said that snow falls are _____ in the mountains.

d Today's newspaper has an _____ about the extinction of some of Canada's birds.

e The telephone technicians checked the _____ beneath the street.

f It's dangerous to ride a _____ on the highway.

g It is very rare to spot a bald _____ .

h A _____ storm damaged houses, demolished haystacks and ruined the wheat crop.

i When Dad was happy he started to _____ his favourite tune.

j It'll take a lot of _____ to move this piano upstairs.

Number Words

6 a Which **mil** word means having a thousand
legs? mil _ _ _ _ _ _

b Which **mil** word means a thousandth of a
gram? mil _ _ _ _ _ _ _

c Which **cent** word means having a hundred
degrees? cent _ _ _ _ _ _ _

d Which **cent** word means a person 100 years
old? cent _ _ _ _ _ _ _ _

e Which **cent** word means a Roman commander of 100
men? cent _ _ _ _ _ _

f Which **cent** word means the one hundredth
year? cent _ _ _ _ _ _

g Which **cent** word means having a hundred
legs? cent _ _ _ _ _ _

h Which **cent** word is a hundredth part of a
metre? cent _ _ _ _ _ _ _

i Which **cent** word means 100 years? cent _ _ _

Find the meaning of millennium and centuple in a dictionary.

An 'LE' Puzzle

7

a A small brown spot on the skin
b Fit to be eaten; eatable
c Able to be seen
d Wise; having good sense
e A long thin piece of paste made from flour, water, and eggs
f An animal with a shell that has paddle-shaped legs and
lives in water
g To wash the throat with liquid by blowing through it at
the back of the mouth
h To move or climb quickly over a rough or steep surface

Unit 22

ough words

> enough plough bough drought
> cough though although dough

1 Write each of the list words in your book. Use each one in a sentence of your own.

2 Unjumble the list words in these sentences and write the sentences in your own book.

- **a** During the storm a (huobg) broke off the tree.
- **b** Is there (hunoeg) food for everyone?
- **c** The (trghdou) caused distress throughout the country.
- **d** In modern bakeries there are large machines that mix the (hguod).
- **e** We will (logpuh) the field ready for the planting of the crops.
- **f** It is quite cold today (glotahuh) the sun is shining brightly.
- **g** Mary had a nasty (ougch) so her mother took her to see the doctor.
- **h** Even (hothug) it's hard work, I enjoy it.

More *ough* Words

3 Find the **ough** words in these sentences and underline them.

- **a** We appreciate your thoughtfulness in sending flowers.
- **b** The police were told to search the house thoroughly.
- **c** She gave the house a thorough cleaning.
- **d** The tunnel is high enough to walk through.
- **e** Throughout his illness, his family visited him in the hospital.
- **f** Although the weather is mild today, spring won't come for two months yet.
- **g** We gave the horses a drink at the water-trough.
- **h** Prices ought to come down soon.
- **i** This horse is a true thoroughbred.
- **j** The shopping centre is located near the main thoroughfare north of the city hall.

4 Use the clues to complete each word.

    a To break up or turn over land _ _**ough**

    b Flour mixed with other dry materials and water for baking _**ough**

    c A long period of very dry weather _ _**ough** _

    d Both these words mean in spite of the fact that _ _**ough** and _ _ _ _**ough**

    e As much as may be necessary _ _**ough**

    f To push air out from the throat suddenly with a rough explosive noise, especially because of discomfort in the lungs _**ough**

    g A branch of a tree _**ough**

N-dings

5 Use the clues to find these 7-letter words that all end in **N**.

a	C						N
b	C						N
c	C						N
d	C						N
e	C						N
f	C						N
g	C						N
h	C						N
i	C						N
j	C						N

charge!

    a A small metal container for carrying water

    b A young hen

    c To interest or trouble yourself with

    d To hold something inside

    e A person who is in charge of a group of people, like soldiers, sailors or a football team

    f A short funny film or a drawing in a newspaper

    g A piece of cloth hanging down to cover a window

    h A group of people travelling together for safety in the desert

    i Carefulness; watchfulness

    j Sure; without any doubt

Compound Words

6 Match a word from List A with a word from List B to make a compound word.

List A	List B	Compound Word
grape	flake	_____
down	house	_____
straw	back	_____
snow	roads	_____
house	fruit	_____
town	work	_____
car	print	_____
horse	stairs	_____
blue	port	_____
cross	berry	

Find the Word

1	2	3	4	5	6	7	8

7 Letters 5, 7,4, 8, 2 means a narrow passage between buildings in cities.

Letters 1, 3, 5, 6 means a thick, flat piece of stone or metal.

The whole is a group of sounds that make a word.

Tricky Words

8 Some everyday words can be hard to spell. Write these *tricky words* into your own book. Make sure you know how to spell them. Use them in sentences of your own.

through	almost
calendar	separate
accept	receive
fierce	scissors
forgotten	escape
onion	edge

Unit 23

ui words

br**ui**se	cr**ui**se	s**ui**t	s**ui**te
n**ui**sance	j**ui**ce	fr**ui**t	q**ui**ver

1 Write each of the list words in your book. Use each one in a sentence of your own.

2 Fill the blanks in these sentences with list words.
  a Every morning with my breakfast I have a glass of orange _____ .
  b That noisy fan is a real _____ .
  c He could tell by the _____ in his lower lip that the child was about to cry.
  d Tchaikovsky's *Nutcracker* _____ is my favourite piece of music.
  e In May, Tate is going on a _____ through the Great Lakes.
  f Stuart wore a sailor _____ to the party.
  g The table overflowed with _____ and vegetables.
  h After her fall on the sidewalk, she noticed a large _____ on her leg.

Six of One; Half a Dozen of the Other

3 The first and last letters are missing from each of the following 6-letter words. Each word begins with the same letter and the final letters, when rearranged, form a word meaning a person's mood or state of mind.

```
—  N D O O —
—  C I C L —
—  N S T E —
—  N F O R —
—  G N I T —
—  N S E C —
```

The jumbled word is_____ .

4 Match the list word with the correct definition.

a A *bruise* is
— a brass instrument like a trumpet
— a small Welsh dog
— a slight injury to the flesh that has discoloured
— an inflamed swelling on the first joint of the big toe

b A *cruise* is
— a fast middle-sized warship
— a sea voyage for pleasure
— the difficult part of a problem
— a group of people who work on a ship

c A *suit* is
— black ash found in a chimney
— a set of clothes intended to be worn together
— something tasting like sugar
— a dangerous fever spread by rats

d *Suite* means
— a number of things making up a set
— the opposite of sour
— an action in a law court
— to change the beat in music

e A *quiver* is
— a case for arrows
— the stiff hollow part of a feather
— a noisy, disorderly crowd
— an angry dispute or argument

f *Juice* is
— a time in tennis when the scores are level
— water containing special minerals that comes from springs underground
— A member of a jury
— The liquid part of fruits and vegetables

Jumbled Words

5 Rearrange the letters to form list words.

tusi   scaeunin
ritfu   uieqvr
rubeis   siurce
cijue   tisue

A 'CO' Puzzle

6 If you use the clues to solve this puzzle, the first column down will give you another **co** word meaning a musical instrument played by blowing into a mouthpiece.

a					C	O			
b			C	O					
c	C				C	O			
d	O				C	O			
e			C	O					
f			C	O					
g			C	O					
h			C	O					

a A coat worn to protect you from rain
b To urge on; to give hope or confidence
c A black substance for drawing made by partly burning wood
d To conquer, defeat, or get the better of
e To know someone again; to acknowledge or admit
f To make beautiful; to adorn
g To meet unexpectedly
h To get back something that was lost, taken away, or stolen

Missing 'E's

7 In each of these words three or four **e's** have been left out. What are the words?

stpl   tnag   btl   xcllnc
rfr   chs   cmtry   fbl
bhiv   lvn   ightn   brz

Unit 24

ei words

> rec**ei**ve **ei**ther n**ei**ther dec**ei**ve c**ei**ling
> conc**ei**t conc**ei**ve h**ei**ght v**ei**l w**ei**gh

1 Write each of the list words in your book. Use each one in a sentence of your own.

2 Fill the blank in each sentence with the correct form of the list word.

 a There was a big _____ for the new ambassador.
 (rec**ei**ve, rec**ei**ver, rec**ei**vable, reception)
 b He _____ me by pretending to be a famous actor.
 (dec**ei**ve, dec**ei**ved, dec**ei**ver, dec**ei**ving)
 c There is no _____ way to raise a thousand dollars.
 (conc**ei**ve, conc**ei**ved, conc**ei**vable, conc**ei**vably)
 d The mountain rises to a _____ of 3000 metres.
 (h**ei**ght, h**ei**ghten, h**ei**ghtened, h**ei**ghtening)
 e A curtain of smog _____ the sun.
 (v**ei**l, v**ei**led, unv**ei**l, unv**ei**ling)
 f The astronauts experienced _____ in space.
 (w**ei**gh, w**ei**ght, w**ei**ghtless, w**ei**ghtlessness)

Confusing Words

3 Use each of the words correctly in a sentence to show that you understand what the word means.

chartered	charted	patent	patient
illegible	eligible	council	counsel
disease	decease	compliment	complement
practise	practice	defective	deficient
stationery	stationary	mythical	mystical

Boxed Words

4 Two list words are jumbled up in each of the boxes below. What are the words? To help you, the <u>first</u> letter of one word and the <u>last</u> letter of the other word are circled.

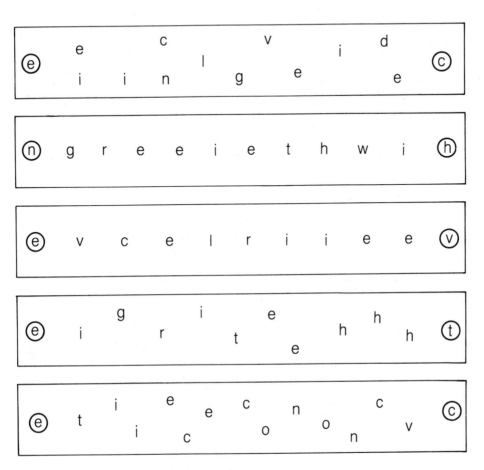

5 Match the clues with the list words.

a	Not one or the other	receive
b	The top of a room	either
c	Too high an opinion of oneself	neither
d	To accept something that is given	deceive
e	The one or the other	ceiling
f	A bride's headdress	conceit
g	To find how heavy something is	conceive
h	The distance to the top	height
i	To mislead by telling lies	veil
j	To form in the mind	weigh

Name the Town

6 Answer each of the clues. Then rearrange the first letter of
each answer to find a town in Nova Scotia.

   a A funny poem with five lines
   b A person who lives nearby
   c Person whose work is putting glass in windows
   d Physical activity; it's good for you
   e A slightly curved yellow fruit with firm, creamy flesh
   f A place where water is collected and stored for use
   g The number above the line in a fraction which shows
      how many parts are taken
   h Not having a job; out of work
   i Bushes, small trees, etc. growing under large trees in
      forests

Word Chains

7 Change ROOM to HEAD and BAND to TUNE in four
moves by changing one letter at a time to form a new
word.

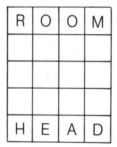

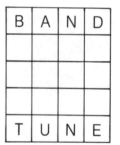

Unit 25

ur words

1   Write each of the list words in your book. Use each one in a sentence of your own.

2   Use the clues to complete each word.

a   Someone who breaks into a house, factory, office, etc. especially at night to steal   _ ur _ _ _ _

b   To break open suddenly; to break into pieces   _ ur _ _

c   To bother or to interrupt   _ _ _ _ ur _

d   A hanging drapery at a window or at the front of a stage   _ ur _ _ _ _

e   Requiring immediate attention or action   ur _ _ _ _

f   A doctor who treats certain injuries and diseases by means of an operation on the damaged part of the body   _ ur _ _ _ _

g   To come upon someone without warning   _ ur _ _ _ _ _

h   To go, or to be, all around   _ ur _ _ _ _ _

i   The outside part of anything   _ ur _ _ _ _

j   The movable articles in a house such as tables, chairs and beds   _ ur _ _ _ur _

Past Tense

3   Fill in the blanks to show the past tense.

a   Today I cruise. Yesterday I _____ .

b   Today he ploughs. Yesterday he _____ .

c   Today I choose. Yesterday I _____ .

d   Today she will speak. Yesterday she _____ .

e   Today Dale will marry Elise. Yesterday Dale _____ Elise.

f   Today Tania writes. Yesterday Tania _____ .

g   Today he whistles. Yesterday he _____ .

h   Today I guard the entrance. Yesterday I _____ the entrance.

4 Fill the blanks in each sentence with the correct form of the list word.

a It is nice to work in pleasant _____ .
(surround, surrounds, surrounded, surroundings)

b The _____ of the sphere is coated with aluminium.
(surface, surfaced, surfacing, resurfaced)

c The outlaws _____ them in the forest.
(surprise, surprised, surprising)

d The house was _____ entirely with handmade items.
(furnish, furnished, furnisher, furniture)

e The _____ took place when no one was at home.
(burgle, burglar, burglary, burgled)

f The riders _____ their horses up the steep hill.
(urge, urged, urgency, urgent)

g Paul has a _____ fitted artificial arm.
(surgeon, surgery, surgical, surgically)

h You can work in here without any _____ .
(disturb, disturbance, disturbed, disturber)

R You Ready?

5 Add an R and rearrange the letters.

a Add R to lace and get a word meaning with nothing in the way so that you can see things clearly.

b Add R to lucy and get a word meaning not straight.

c Add R to sags and get a low green plant that covers fields and lawns.

d Add R to pace and get a word meaning to leap or jump about happily.

e Add R to ace and get a worry or a trouble.

f Add R to bug and get a soft, fat new-born insect.

g Add R to tile and get a measurement of capacity.

h Add R to sham and get a piece of wet swampy ground.

i Add R to title and get garbage or waste paper left lying about.

j Add R to steam and get someone who is very skilled at a particular craft.

Antonyms

6 Match each word in List A with its antonym (opposite) in List B.

List A
fail
hide
damage
obey
remember
rude
offer
punish
divide
known

List B
polite
unknown
succeed
reward
receive
repair
multiply
disobey
forget
reveal

Sub Words

7 The prefix **sub** usually means **under** or **below**. Add it to these words and use each one in a sentence.

way	marine	standard
ordinate	lime	divide
title	scribe	merge
urban	conscious	tract
due	side	tropical

PH or *GH* or *FF* or *F*

8 Complete each word with the correct group of letters. All have the 'f' sound.

ne ___ ew	sni ___	or ___ an
blu ___	autogra ___	cou ___
co ___ ee	tou ___	di ___ erent
gra ___ ite	al ___ abet	proo ___
rou ___	___ antom	si ___ on
o ___ er	enou ___	o ___ ice
chie ___	com ___ ort	lau ___ ter

Unit 26

au words

autograph	audience	author	automatic	authority
laundry	launch	cautious	gauze	exhausted

1 Write each of the list words in your book. Use each one in a sentence of your own.

2 Unjumble the list words in these sentences.

   a Breathing and blinking are (citmouata) reactions.
   b A leading agricultural (ytthiauor) predicts that the price of wheat will fall.
   c Be (suoituac) when swimming in deep water.
   d The campers' supply of food was (shudeexat).
   e Our word (narlyud) comes from the Latin *lavare* meaning 'to wash'.
   f When I broke my arm my teacher signed her (paguratoh) on my cast.
   g The nurse changed the (zeaug) on the patient's leg.
   h Pierre Berton is in Vancouver this week to (hnulac) his new book.
   i Mark Twain is the (tahuor) of *Tom Sawyer*.
   j The (edaueicn) applauded the performance.

3 Write four words for each of these.

-ang	str-	-ung	per-
_____	_____	_____	_____
_____	_____	_____	_____
_____	_____	_____	_____
_____	_____	_____	_____

4 Use the clues to complete each word.

   a A thin transparent fabric   _ au _ _
   b A person's own signature or handwriting
      au _ _ _ _ _ _
   c The power or right which a person may have and exercise because of his position
      au _ _ _ _ _ _

d Tired out or used up _ _ _ **au** _ _ _ _ .

e An assembly of people who listen or watch
au _ _ _ _ _ _

f To start something on its way. Also a large power-driven boat _ **au** _ _ _

g Careful; watchful _ **au** _ _ _ _ _

h Self-moving; working of itself **au** _ _ _ _ _ _ _ _

i A place where clothes are washed and ironed
_ **au** _ _ _ _

j The writer of a book, play, article, etc. **au** _ _ _ _

Word Pyramid

5 Use the letters **A**, **N**, and **T** at least once in each row to form seven words.

Antonyms and Synonyms

6 Write **A** or **S** to show whether the two words are antonyms or synonyms.

accept	reject	_	timidity	audacity	_
struggle	tussle	_	devout	religious	_
copy	emulate	_	infiltrate	penetrate	_
industrious	idle	_	alert	drowsy	_
temporary	permanent	_	conceit	vanity	_

ance or *ence*

7 Complete these words using **ance** or **ence**.

adv _ _ _ _   ignor _ _ _ _   abs _ _ _ _

observ _ _ _ _   viol _ _ _ _   inst _ _ _ _

influ _ _ _ _   audi _ _ _ _   excell _ _ _ _

resid _ _ _ _   abund _ _ _ _   sequ _ _ _ _

eleg _ _ _ _   interfer _ _ _ _   confid _ _ _ _

Numbers

8 Write the words for each ordinal number.

4th _____   11th _____   12th _____

13th _____   14th _____   20th _____

29th _____   30th _____   40th _____

80th _____   69th _____   53rd _____

22nd _____   3rd _____   71st _____

Confusing Words

9 Use each word in a short sentence.

quality	quantity	weary	wary
rhyme	rhythm	hanger	hangar
farther	further	heaven	haven
bought	brought	trail	trial
hoard	horde	mould	moult

Whisper whisper

Find the Word

1	2	3	4	5	6	7

10 Letters 5, 6, 1, 6, 7 is a punctuation mark and is also the greater part of the large intestine.
Letters 2, 3, 5, 2, 1 means to be better than others at something; to do well.
The whole word is a dictionary.

Unit 27

ure words

tort**ure**	agricult**ure**	press**ure**	depart**ure**	leis**ure**
fract**ure**	past**ure**	punct**ure**	enclos**ure**	signat**ure**

1 Write each of the list words in your book. Use each one in a sentence of your own.

2 Complete each sentence with a list word.

   a During my _____ time I like to read.
   b The cattle were herded into a small _____.
   c Better methods of _____ are needed to feed the world's population.
   d Waiting for news of the lost boy was sheer _____ to his parents.
   e The Minister of Trade wrote his _____ at the bottom of the treaty.
   f A _____ in the balloon made it collapse.
   g Having to cope with so many problems put him under great _____.
   h When Terezia fell, she suffered a _____ of her wrist.
   i Our _____ is scheduled for 6 a.m. tomorrow.
   j The cattle were put out to _____ to fatten them for the market.

Double Letters

3

fina __ __ y	f __ __ lish	co __ __ ect
co __ __ ode	ke __ __ el	i __ __ ne __ __
swo __ __ en	co __ __ er	pu __ __ le
po __ __ en	usua __ __ y	le __ __ on
hu __ __ le	sh __ __ r	ri __ __ le
gra __ __ ho __ __ er	tra __ __ ic	ye __ __ ow

4 Use the clues to complete each word.

a   Something shut in, such as land surrounded by a fence _ _ _ _ _ _ **—ure**

b   To inflict great pain on a person as a punishment or to try to force a confession _ _ _ _**—ure**

c   A signed name. Also in music the flats and sharps that show the key _ _ _ _ _ _ **—ure**

d   Spare time; time free from employment _ _ _ _ **—ure**

e   A going away or leaving _ _ _ _ _ _ _ **—ure**

f   The cultivation of the land _ _ _ _ _ _ _ _ **—ure**

g   To pierce or prick with a sharp point _ _ _ _ _ **—ure**

h   The breaking of a bone or something hard _ _ _ _ _ **—ure**

i   A strong influence; a pressing force _ _ _ _ _ **—ure**

j   A piece of land with growing grass for cattle and sheep to feed on _ _ _ _ **—ure**

Antonyms

5 Match each word in List A with its antonym in List B.

	List A	**List B**
a	separate	commence
b	welcome	answer
c	grateful	dislike
d	admire	improper
e	cease	combine
f	shout	unwelcome
g	delightful	whisper
h	proper	sensible
i	question	ungrateful
j	foolish	unpleasant

6 Write 3 list words that can be made from these letters:

S S S T L P E E R R O I T U R E U R E U R E

Synonyms

7 Match each word in the first box with its synonym in the second box.

> supply   beautiful   depart
> dawn   eager   jetty   usual
> annoy   cargo   remark

> leave   pier   comment
> common   attractive   provide   sunrise
> keen   irritate   freight

Words From People's Names

8 Match the words in the box with the people they are associated with. Then find the meaning of each word in a dictionary.

> galvanize   morse   wellingtons
> bunsen burner   watt   volt

a This unit was named after James Watt (1736–1819), the Scottish engineer who pioneered the development of the steam engine. The word is _____ and it means _____.

b This footwear was named after the first Duke of Wellington (1769–1852), the British general who defeated Napoleon at the Battle of Waterloo. The word is _____ and it means _____.

c This process was named after an Italian scientist, Luigi Galvani (1737–98). The word is _____ and it means _____.

d This unit was also named after an Italian scientist who lived around the same time as Galvani, Alessandro Volta (1745–1827). The word is _____ and it means _____.

e This object found in many science classrooms was named after Robert W. Bunsen, the German chemist who invented it. The word is _____ and it means _____.

f This code was named after the American inventor of the telegraph, Samuel F. B. Morse (1791–1872). The word is _____ and it means _____.

Unit 28

y = 'i' words

dye lying supply pygmy mystery
rhythm cygnet pyramid crystal myth

1   Write each of the list words in your book. Use each one in
a sentence of your own.

Which Word To Use?

2   Fill the blanks in each sentence with the correct form of the
list word.

    a   The French painters often used historical and _____
subjects.
(myth, mythical, mythology, mythologist)

    b   His thoughts had not yet _____ .
(crystal, crystals, crystalline, crystallized)

    c   The _____ sound of the waves lapping against the
shore was very peaceful.
(rhythm, rhythmic, rhythmical, rhythmically)

    d   There is something _____ about those people.
(mystery, mysteries, mysterious, mysteriously)

    e   What _____ will we need for our climb?
(supply, supplies, supplied, supplier)

    f   The town _____ north of here.
(lie, lies, lying, lain)

Jumbled Words

3   Rearrange the letters to form list words.

tersymy	thym
giyln	dey
tnycge	dmrpyai
lryctas	mtyrhh
plyusp	gmyyp

4 Match the list words with the correct definitions.

a *Dye* is
— to stop living
— one of a pair of dice
— a substance used to colour something
— all of the above

b A *cygnet* is
— a type of ring worn on the fourth finger
— an abbreviated signature
— a male goose
— a young swan

c *Crystal* is
— a clear transparent mineral like sparkling glass
— a roller-shaped object, either hollow or solid
— a solid black mineral used as fuel
— a closely woven heavy silk

d A *myth* is
— a charm supposed to have magic powers for the wearer
— a story about heroes or gods of ancient times; a fable
— a kind of resin with a bitter taste, used in some medicines
— a tiny green flowerless plant that grows in patches that are moist.

e A *pyramid* is
— a figure with three angles and three sides
— a solid square with six equal square faces
— a solid body whose two ends are the same shape and size
— a solid shape with a triangle on each of three sides and a base, meeting in a point at the top

Correct Endings

5 Place **ary, ory, ury** or **ery** into the correct spaces.

anniversary _ _ _   batt _ _ _   cel _ _ _
arch _ _ _   dormit _ _ _   forg _ _ _
cemet _ _ _   brew _ _ _   conservat _ _ _
extraordin _ _ _   bak _ _ _   imagin _ _ _
f _ _ _   rook _ _ _   inj _ _ _
pott _ _ _   nurs _ _ _   prim _ _ _
cent _ _ _   cutl _ _ _   laborat _ _ _
gall _ _ _   jewell _ _ _   satisfact _ _ _

'Re' Words

6 The prefix **re** usually means *again* or *back*. Add it to these words and use each one in a sentence.

place   collect   form
assure   organize   verse
arrange   produce   bound
tail   new   trace
coil   serve   store
allocate   claim   capture

Six of One; Half a Dozen of the Other

7 The first and last letters are missing from each of the following 6-letter words. Each word begins with the same letter, and the final letters when rearranged form a word meaning to interfere with what someone is trying to do.

_ A G G E _
_ O V I A _
_ A I L E _
_ U G G L _
_ E T S A _
_ U M B L _

The jumbled word is _____.

Unit 29

---

collar harbour separate guard library
secretary harvest similar carnival vinegar

---

1 Write each of the list words in your book. Use each one in a sentence of your own.

2 Fill the blank in each sentence with the correct form of the list word.

    a The cabin cruiser was safely _____ during the storm.
       (harbour, harbourage, harboured, harbouring)

    b Their _____ at the railway station was very sad.
       (separate, separable, separation, separator)

    c The entrance was _____ by two ferocious dogs.
       (guard, guards, guarded, guarding)

    d In our city there are three _____.
       (library, library's, libraries, librarian)

    e Lee is doing a _____ course at the college.
       (secretary, secretaries, secretarial, secretariat)

    f There's a strong _____ between those two paintings.
       (similar, similarity, similarities, similarly)

3 Match the clues with the list words.

    a A building containing a collection of books

    b To protect from danger or attack

    c A sour-tasting liquid made from cider

    d Something worn round the neck

    e A person who deals with correspondence, records, etc.

    f A festival

    g A port for ships

    h Like or almost alike

    i The time of gathering ripened crops

    j To set apart; to divide

collar
harbour
separate
guard
library
secretary
harvest
vinegar
similar
carnival

Name the City

4 Answer each of the clues. Then rearrange the first letter of each answer to make a Canadian city.

 a An Australian animal with strong hind legs for jumping
 b A summer shoe that is held to the foot by straps
 c The great mass of salt water that covers two-thirds of the world's surface
 d The lower part of the human body that contains the stomach and intestines
 e Hard fat used for making candles and soap
 f The sport of shooting with bows and arrows
 g A dish containing eggs that are beaten and cooked in a pan
 h Something needed for life and growth; food
 i A cloth or leather sports shoe with a rubber sole

The city is _ _ _ _ _ _ _ _ _.

Missing 'E's

5 In each of these words three or four **e's** have been left out. What are the words?

ri	ndl
btwn	flr
crpr	bvrag
xrcis	dgr
flc	rvrs
mssngr	dcas

Synonyms

6 Match each word in the first box with its synonym in the second box.

> afraid   garbage   weary
> illness   bravery   wound   cruel
> happen   wander   inspect

> tired   sickness   unkind
> examine   injury   scared   occur
> refuse   courage   stroll

Confusing Words

7 Use each of these words correctly in a sentence to show that you understand what the word means.

prosecute	persecute	prescription	inscription
essay	assay	fluent	fluid
between	among	die	dye
septic	sceptic	pedal	peddle
leaned	lent	yoke	yolk

Missing Vowels

8 Complete each word by adding the vowels.

bsbll	cmr	clnt
drgn	scp	fmn
gllnt	gttr	hv
hldy	ntrdc	lcrc
mrthn	mldw	nphw
pstr	ppl	rqst
shltr	tp	wtr
yth	pblc	bndn

Unit 30

Review

1 Choose the correct word.

a	wistle	whistle	whistel
b	bycycle	bicycel	bicycle
c	enough	enugh	enugh
d	nuisance	newsance	nuisence
e	kwiver	qiver	quiver
f	receeve	receive	recieve
g	sirprise	surprize	surprise
h	surgon	surgeon	surgoen
i	garze	gauze	gause
j	decieve	deceive	deceeve
k	allthority	orthority	authority
l	puncture	punkture	punctore
m	mith	mythe	myth
n	collar	colar	coller
o	rvthm	rhythm	rihythm
p	burgular	burglar	burgler

2 Write these words into your book and group them into *word families*.

urgent	possible	cough
bruise	autograph	cygnet
cruise	either	cable
torture	pyramid	conceive
furniture	harvest	laundry
probable	drought	crystal
enclosure	juice	leisure
exhausted	ceiling	although
disturb	vinegar	similar

3 Find the small words that are in the larger words.

whistle	neither	surround
urgent	harvest	drought
pyramid	bicycle	juice
probable	height	surface
agriculture	vinegar	signature

Jumbled Words

4 Unjumble each word. Then write the plural for each word.
The first one has been done for you.

a	yde	dye	dyes
b	aglee	____	____
c	oeursgn	____	____
d	goluph	____	____
e	cualnh	____	____
f	iubsre	____	____
g	nleciig	____	____
h	yirhaoutt	____	____
i	ertsapu	____	____
j	mgyyp	____	____
k	rrlbiay	____	____
l	dragu	____	____
m	cclbeyi	____	

Mixed Words

5 Each group of letters contains two words from Units 21 to
29. What are the words?

Example: g   u   a   r d   = guard
          ↑   ↑   ↑   ↑↑
       g d i u s t a u r d r b
          ↓↓   ↓↓ ↓   ↓↓
          d i s t u   r b = disturb

rqespuonsiivbleer	cmuryttaihn
mfuuscrnliteure	cbautoiuogush
aaultothmoautghic	dreepartceureive
enxuihsaanucsteed	mayrsteticryle
ftrearrctibulree	scecrabelteary
scuoincteite	cbarniurvsalt

A Jumbo Word Search

6 How many words from Units 21 to 29 can you find in this word search? The words go across the page and down the page.

```
S U R R O U N D A B E A
C S E A G L E D E F X U
M U S C L E I M Y T H T
B P P R A U T H O R A O
I P O U G L H C O N U G
C L N I D S E Y O E S R
Y Y S S T U R G E N T A
C D I E O R N N M O E P
L R B E R G L E B U D H
E O L G T E O T U G R Q
S U E A U O N E P H I U
U G F U R N I T U R E I
I H O Z E J U I C E F V
T T R E E C O L L A R E
E B B Y I A B L E M U R
P R O B A B L E A P I I
O E U R R L V E I L T P
S C G U T E R R I B L E
S E H I I S O A P U N N
I I O S C S Z T Y R E O
B V R E L Y I N G G V U
L E S H E I G H T L I G
E V E S T B F L A A N H
A G R I C U L T U R E X
S N M G A R A W E I G H
U U C N P S P D A F A P
I I O A L T S O A T R R
T S U T P L O U G H P E
A A G U A R D G I S Y S
L N H R E A M H N U G S
T C C E I L I N G N M U
H E A R L A U N D R Y R
O U T X A U D I E N C E
U N C L E N T H O U G H
G O F R A C T U R E E L
H A R D W H I S T L E N
```

Unit 31

ue words

tong**ue**   fatig**ue**   plag**ue**   synagog**ue**   catalog**ue** league   vag**ue**   rev**ue**   c**ue**   morg**ue**

1   Write each of the list words in your book. Use each one in a sentence of your own.

Proofreading

2   Correct the spelling mistakes in these sentences.

  a   The docter tolled me to stik out my tounge.
  b   I felt grate fatige after climming the steep hill.
  c   In the forteenth sentury the plague killed one-third of the popalation of Europe.
  d   On saterday they went to the synagog.
  e   If you want to use the libary you shoold no how to use the computer caterlogue.
  f   Several nations formed a defence leegue.
  g   The strangor was rather vage about his parst.
  h   This year's review at the thaetre was not very good.
  i   A que is another name four a billards stick.
  j   After the accedent the bodie was taken to the morge.

Jumbled Letters

3   Rearrange the letters to form list words.

gaveu   uaelpg
ruvee   uaelge
euc   tiafuge
ugolatace   ugosegyna
euromg   egnotu

Antonyms

4 Match each word in List A with its antonym in List B.

List A	List B
bitter	simple
faithful	shallow
wrap	sweet
fresh	infamous
deep	release
famous	stale
trap	humble
attack	unfaithful
difficult	unwrap
proud	defend

5 Write four words for each of these.

-mps **spr-** **-ear** **-our**

_____ _____ _____ _____
_____ _____ _____ _____
_____ _____ _____ _____
_____ _____ _____ _____

Down the Ladder

6 Use the clues to move down the **IS** ladder.

a Land surrounded by water
b To give attention in hearing
c A metal tool with a sharp edge at the end of a blade, used for cutting into or shaping wood, stone, etc.
d Having prejudice against someone on the basis of gender
e The bowl-shaped frame of bones at the base of the backbone

a	I	S				
b		I	S			
c			I	S		
d				I	S	
e					I	S

SO Words

7 Use the clues to find these words that all contain the letters **SO**

					S	O		
a					S	O		
b				S	O			
c	S	O						
d				S	O			
e				S	O			
f				S	O			
g				S	O			
h	S	O						

a The flowers on fruit trees and shrubs
b An event in a story; a complete short story that is part of a longer story
c The state of being alone; by yourself
d Someone who has been captured in war
e Private; one's own
f A cutting tool like two knives fastened together in the middle
g To add things like salt and pepper to food to improve the flavour
h Serious or very earnest

Did You Know?

8 The word *sandwich* is named after the man who invented it. John Montague, the Earl of Sandwich, would sit for hours and hours playing cards with his friends. One day he was so busy playing that he did not want to stop for lunch. He told his servant to bring him some meat, and to put it between two pieces of bread so that the cards would not get greasy. And so today, food between slices of bread is called a sandwich — named after the Earl of Sandwich.

Unit 32

---

promise   practise   excuse   course   coarse
tease   rouse   appease   nonsense   else

---

1   Write each of the list words in your book. Use each one in a sentence of your own.

2   Complete these sentences with list words.

a   The worker had rough, _____ hands.
b   Mom said 'You had better tidy your bedroom or _____!'
c   Don't _____ the cat or it will scratch you.
d   I _____ that I'll never do that again.
e   Nothing would _____ the crying baby.
f   If you're going to talk _____, we can't discuss this problem.
g   Vicky said she would _____ the piano every night.
h   The ship was 200 kilometres off _____.
i   We could not _____ Marty from his sound sleep.
j   Please _____ me for interrupting.

3   Match the word with the definition.

a   Speech or writing with no meaning   promise
b   The path over which something   practise
    moves   excuse
c   To waken   course
d   To give one's word   coarse
e   To calm or pacify someone   tease
f   To put into action   rouse
g   Otherwise, if not   appease
h   To annoy a person   nonsense
i   A reason given for not doing   else
    something
j   Rough or rude

Synonyms

4 Match each word in the first box with its synonym in the
second box.

> choose   assist   finish
> gentle   begin   cheer   gather
> fierce   depend   enemy

> help   commence   wild
> applaud   rely   collect   foe
> select   timid   complete

Past Tense

5 Fill in the blanks to show the past tense.

   a Today I will tear the paper into small pieces.
      Yesterday I _____ the paper.

   b Today Raja will begin to write a new book.
      Yesterday Raja _____ writing a new book.

   c Today Pierre will weave a rug from the wool.
      Yesterday Pierre _____ a rug.

   d Tomorrow I will rise at six o'clock.
      Yesterday I _____ at six o'clock.

   e Today Megan will try to shrink her baggy jeans.
      Yesterday Megan _____ her baggy jeans.

   f Today Naomi will freeze as she hasn't a coat.
      Yesterday Naomi _____ when the temperature
      dropped.

   g Today Ahmed will cling to the side of the pool.
      Yesterday Ahmed _____ to the side.

A 'CO' Puzzle

6 If you use the clues to solve this puzzle, the first column down will give you another **co** word which is a fruit.

a			C	O					
b						C	O		
c			C	O					
d			C	O					
e				C	O				
f				C	O				
g					C	O			

a A statement of money received and spent
b A garment worn beneath a dress
c To set down in writing so as to keep for future use
d Money that comes in from business, property, work, etc.
e A large reptile with a long body, four short legs, a thick skin and a long tail
f A coat worn in cold weather over other clothes
g An instrument for making distant objects appear nearer and larger

Ring Word

7 Look at the letters below and see if you can find the 9-letter word hiding there. Start anywhere, but use each letter once only and move along the lines connecting the circles.

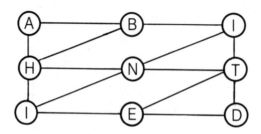

Unit 33

ee words

steeple   referee   jamboree   fleece   reindeer
volunteer   proceed   exceed   eerie   beetle

1 Write each of the list words in your book. Use each one in a sentence of your own.

Boxed Words

2 Two list words are jumbled up in each of the boxes below. What are the words? To help you, the <u>first</u> letter of one word and the <u>last</u> letter of the other word are circled.

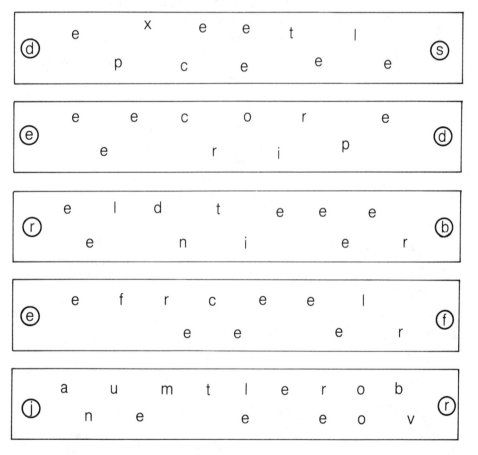

3 Write the list words in alphabetical order.

4 Match the list word with the correct definition.

a A *steeple* is
— a long thin sword used in fencing
— a small shellfish
— a high tower on a church
— a drink containing alcohol

b A *referee* is
— an umpire in certain sports
— a race for yachts
— a tube for drawing liquid out of a container
— a written law of a country

c A *jamboree* is
— a jam made from the leaves of the boree plant
— Australian slang for a flock of sheep
— a large gathering of scouts

d A *fleece* is
— a number of ships together
— a sheep's coat of wool
— a hard kind of stone
— the side of an animal

e *Eerie* means
— covered with thick hair
— foggy, misty
— a feeling of sickness
— weird; causing fear

f *Proceed* means
— dull; uninteresting
— to go on; to continue
— a side view of a face or head
— to free from danger or captivity

Name the City

5 Answer each of the clues. Then rearrange the first letter of each answer to make a city in New Brunswick.

 a   A plant with a prickly stalk and leaves. The national flower of Scotland
 b   Sound that leaves make when moved by the wind
 c   A school of higher learning
 d   An event not wanted, intended, or planned to happen
 e   A listing of events
 f   A process that combines pictures and sounds
 g   An ocean fish related to the cod
 h   One of the main branches of a tree

a
b
c
d
e
f
g
h

The city is _____ .

Correct Endings

6 Complete these words with **ar, er** or **or**

sol __ __   compos __ __   peculi __ __
advis __ __   angul __ __   orat __ __
simil __ __   auth __ __   creat __ __
lun __ __   murder __ __   regul __ __
jewell __ __   offic __ __   solicit __ __
debt __ __   arch __ __   propell __ __

Unit 34

ea words

| measure | pleasant | pleasure | breakfast | league |
| decrease | appeal | theatre | reveal | conceal |

1 Write each of the list words in your book. Use each one in a sentence of your own.

2 Fill the blanks in each sentence with the correct form of the list word.

   a What are the _____ of the window?
(measure, measured, measurements)
   b The gift gave the child a great deal of _____.
(pleasure, pleasant, pleasurable)
   c The different teams joined together to form a baseball

      _____.
(league, leagued, leaguing)
   d The number of children at our school is _____.
(decrease, decreased, decreasing)
   e Mr Kahn was the _____ in the court case.
(appeal, appealing, appellant)
   f Anissa comes from a _____ family.
(theatre, theatrical, theatrically)
   g 'Spilling the beans' means confessing or making a
startling _____.
(reveal, revealed, revelation)
   h The boy remained in _____ until the bully went away.
(conceal, concealing, concealment)

3 Write all of the list words in alphabetical order.

ent or *ant*

4 Complete these words by adding either **ent** or **ant**

obedi _ _ _   import _ _ _   entr _ _ _
perman _ _ _   inhabit _ _ _   pleas _ _ _
eleg _ _ _   contin _ _ _   conveni _ _ _
frequ _ _ _   ignor _ _ _   independ _ _ _
fragr _ _ _   viol _ _ _   dist _ _ _

R You Ready?

5 Add an **R** and rearrange the letters.

a   Add **R** to <u>vile</u> and get an inside part of the body.
b   Add **R** to <u>rode</u> and get a command.
c   Add **R** to <u>time</u> and get a word meaning to deserve something such as a reward.
d   Add **R** to <u>semi</u> and get someone who hoards all his money and lives in a very poor way.
e   Add **R** to <u>leap</u> and get a small, creamy-white jewel used for <u>necklaces</u> and other jewellery.
f   Add **R** to <u>even</u> and get a word meaning not at any time.
g   Add **R** to opal and get a word meaning having to do with the <u>North</u> and South Poles.
h   Add **R** to <u>tote</u> and get a furry, web-footed swimming animal.
i   Add **R** to <u>date</u> and get a word meaning to buy and sell; to exchange.
j   Add **R** to <u>pile</u> and get a word meaning great danger.

Make a Word

6 Make 3 list words using these letters.

aaaa   pp g
cc   n   o
eeee lll   u

Missing 'E's

7 In each of these words three or four **e's** have been left out. What are the words?

clbrat   lswhr
dcras   dpn
frz   dfnc
krosn   rsrv
vrgrn   ndl
nginr   rciv

An 'M' Puzzle

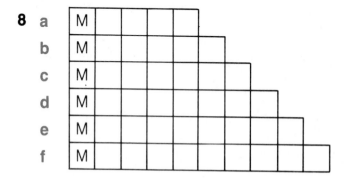

8 a
b
c
d
e
f

a A grinding tooth
b Small fungi found on leather, cloth, etc. which is damp
c A ruler
d A fungus that grows quickly and can be eaten
e Small-scale, such as a small-scale model
f Always the same; dull

In Words

9 The prefix **in** usually means *not*. Add it to these words and use each one in a sentence.

justice   firm   capable
convenient   decent   digestible
soluble   flexible   credible
correct   activity   valuable
accurate   complete   distinct

Unit 35

Soft 'c' words

silence decide accident science century
bicycle electricity centre niece piece

1 Write each of the list words in your book. Use each one in a sentence of your own.

2 Fill the blanks in each sentence with the correct form of the list word.

    a The gangster used a _____ on the end of his gun.
       (silence, silencer, silent)
    b We've _____ to buy a house in the country.
       (decide, decided, deciding)
    c The breaking of the window was _____ .
       (accident, accidentally, accidental)
    d The _____ spent hours in the laboratory.
       (scientist, scientific, scientifically)
    e When our stove wasn't working, we called an _____ .
       (electrician; electric; electricity)
    f With the new T.V. set the picture had to be _____ .
       (centre, centring, centred)

ible or able

3 Place the correct ending, either **ible** or **able** in the blanks.

respons __ __ __ __   excus __ __ __ __
const __ __ __ __   service __ __ __ __ __
advis __ __ __ __   mov __ __ __ __
inevit __ __ __ __   cred __ __ __ __
hospit __ __ __ __   terr __ __ __ __
depend __ __ __ __   valu __ __ __ __
favour __ __ __ __   miser __ __ __ __
irrit __ __ __ __   present __ __ __ __
vis __ __ __ __   replace __ __ __ __
cap __ __ __ __   convert __ __ __ __
invis __ __ __ __   manage __ __ __ __
accept __ __ __ __   gull __ __ __ __

104

Synonyms

4 Match each word in the first box with its synonym in the second box.

> strange   join   change
> famous   sure   crack   scared
> journey   pitch   repair

> combine   throw   renowned
> certain   frightened   mend   trip
> unfamiliar   alter   split

Confusing Words

5 Use each of these words correctly in a sentence to show that you understand what the word means.

larva	lava	gambol	gamble
idle	idol	manner	manor
coarse	course	sighs	size
lightning	lightening	scull	skull
desert	dessert	barque	bark
sealing	ceiling	mustard	mustered
coral	choral	chord	cord
mussel	muscle	hoard	horde
serial	cereal	faint	feint

6 Write four words for each of these.

-dge   **con-**   **-ity**   **pro-**

Number Words

7 **a** Which **quad** word means having four legs?

quad __ __ __ __ __

b Which **dec** word means proceeding by tens?

dec __ __ __ __

c Which **quin** word means one group of five?   quin __ __ __

d Which **quad** word means one of four children?   quad __ __ __ __ __ __

e Which **quad** word means a geometric figure with four sides?   quad __ __ __ __ __ __

f Which **oct** word means an eight-sided shape?

oct __ __ __ __

g Which **pent** word means a five-sided shape?

pent __ __ __ __

h Which **pent** word means an athletics contest where each competitor takes part in five events?

pent __ __ __ __ __ __

i Which **oct** word is a sea creature with eight 'arms'?   oct __ __ __ __

Find the meaning of these words in a dictionary

pentameter	octave	quadrant
octavo	decimate	octogenarian

Missing 'i's

8 These words have three or more **i's** missing. Write out the correct words in your books.

cvlan	ntal	dscplne
nfnty	nvsble	mllonare
nvtng	cvlzaton	lmtaton

Word Chains

9 Change SHORE to SCOUT and CRACK to CRONE in 3 moves by changing one letter at a time to make a new word.

S	H	O	R	E
S	C	O	U	T

C	R	A	C	K
C	R	O	N	E

Unit 36

Silent 'g' words

gnash	gnaw	gnarled	gnat	sign
resign	campaign	reign	design	champagne

1 Write each of the list words in your book. Use each one in a sentence of your own.

2 Fill the blanks in these sentences with list words.

   a At work my father is trying to _____ a new generator to save his company a lot of money.

   b I asked the champion skater if she would _____ my autograph book.

   c I watched the young child _____ his teeth together in anger.

   d When the _____ bit me it left a red lump on my arm.

   e Next week my mother will begin her _____ for re-election to the City Council.

   f The last time Mom was elected to Council we celebrated with _____.

   g That _____ oak tree is a hundred years old.

   h My sister will often _____ on a crunchy apple while watching television.

   i Robin Hood is said to have lived during the _____ of King Richard the Lionheart.

   j Dad had to _____ from the School Council because he couldn't get to the meetings any more.

3 Which three list words can you make from these letters?

RAAEI D S CEIEH
GGMP G N NN

4 Match the list word with the correct definition.

a *Gnaw* means
— not one or the other
— to bite in a continuous scraping manner
— to swallow food quickly
— to lift something with great effort

b *Gnarled* means
— twisted; knotty
— angry; furious
— to shake or stir up
— to separate by force

c A *campaign* is
— a series of military operations in one area of a war
— an organized series of meetings, speeches, etc.
— a planned series of advertisements in the press or on television
— all of the above

d *Resign* means
— to move back or go away
— to search for and fetch
— to make a sharp or witty reply
— to give up your position or employment

e *Champagne* is
— a South American lizard that changes colour
— a dealer in candles and oil
— a wine, usually white and sparkling
— a person who has defeated all others in a sport

A King Kong Puzzle

5 Use the letters **A, P** and **E** at least once in each row to form seven words

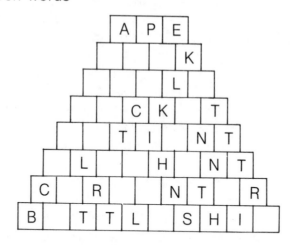

Antonyms

6 Match each word in List A with its antonym in List B.

List A	**List B**
straight	completion
beautiful	unable
excited	displease
usual	loser
beginning	similar
please	crooked
winner	unusual
different	insincere
sincere	ugly
able	calm

A Puzzle

7 The last four letters of these words are jumbled. What are the words?

stoareg	tileck	vioisn
gaaxly	icleic	maerkt
poluelt	reeucs	steleni
algne	bchea	brocureh
caerer	hurgne	gielgg
faltuy	exripe	dawr

Unit 37

per words

perform	performance	perhaps	permission
perfect	percentage	perspire	persuade.

1   Write each of the list words in your book. Use each one in a sentence of your own.

2   Write the eight list words in your book and beside each one write a definition for that word. Use a dictionary to help you.
       Now find the meanings of these other per words.

perceive	perforate	permit
perspective	perpetual	perception
perfume	permanent	perennial
persecute	perimeter	persist

Proofreading

3   Correct the spelling mistakes in these sentences.

     a   May I have permision to youse the pensil sharpener?
     b   Can you draw a purrfect sircle?
     c   A skiled worker can preform the taske easily.
     d   The theater gives too performences a day.
     e   Can't we perswade you to cum to the party?
     f   The marathon runers began to purspire during the rase
     g   Perhapes it will reign tonight.
     h   A large persentage of the cars had a falt in the breaks.

An 'S' Puzzle

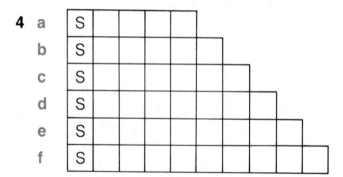

4

a Having to do with the sun
b To turn aside quickly from a direct course
c A word having the same (or nearly the same) meaning as another word
d Deliberate destruction or malicious damage to machinery, property, etc.
e The right side of a ship when facing towards the front (the bow)
f The apparatus fixed to the wheels of a car to lessen the effects of rough road surfaces

Double Letters

5 Complete each word with a double letter.

begi __ __ ing   inte __ __ upt   co __ __ on
co __ __ and   stru __ __ le   e __ __ ect
gi __ __ le   mu __ __ le   pa __ __ enger
a __ __ ist   tu __ __ el   a __ __ re __ __
ca __ __ age   su __ __ ly   le __ __ uce
nece __ __ ary   sci __ __ ors   te __ __ ible

Did You Know?

6 Our word *ear* comes from an old English word that was pronounced like **air**. The Latin word for **ear** is *auris* and from this we get words such as audition, audience and audible.

    An audition is a trial hearing of actors or singers to see if they are good enough to take part in a show. An audience is a group of people who listen to a show. Audible means something that can be heard.

A 'CO' Puzzle

7 Use the clues to complete this puzzle.

		C	O			
a		C	O			
b					C	O
c				C	O	
d	C	O				
e				C	O	
f				C	O	
g				C	O	
h				C	O	

a A small two-wheeled vehicle moved by pushing with one foot

b A plant with large leaves which are dried and used in cigarettes

c An imaginary horse-like animal with a horn on its forehead

d To guide; to lead; to be in charge

e To greet someone with joy

f A small flute

g A large bird with beautifully-coloured feathers

h A special kind of corn that bursts open when it is heated

Per Sentences

8 Write these sentences in your book using the correct **per** word.

a The witness lied to the jury and was charged with (perjury, permeate).

b The athlete was in (perfect, perturb) health.

c Despite hardships, she (persuaded, persisted) in her efforts to get a university education.

d An entertainer has to have a lot of (personality, perspective).

e (Permissive, perishable) foods must be kept refrigerated.

Unit 38

ge words.

privilege	ravage	beverage	engage	courage
postage	average	change	college	marriage

1 Write each of the list words in your book. Use each one in a sentence of your own.

2 Fill the blanks in each sentence with the correct form of the list word.

    a The invaders _____ the countryside.
    (ravage, ravaged, ravager, ravaging)
    b The movie star led a _____ life.
    (privilege, privileged, privileges)
    c The couple announced their _____ at the party.
    (engage, engaged, engagement, engaging)
    d Keep me _____ on the situation.
    (post, posted, postage postal)
    e During the race the motorcycles were _____ speeds of 160 kilometres per hour.
    (average, averaged, averaging)
    f His moods are as _____ as the weather.
    (change, changeable, changing)
    g She _____ a man from her home town.
    (marry, marriage, married, marriageable)

Word Square

3 List as many words as you can from the letters in the word square. Each word must be made up of letters in squares which touch each other.

S	E	R	E
A	V	A	N
T	O	G	D
S	S	E	L

N-dings

4 Use the clues to find these words that all end in N

a	P					N	
b	P					N	
c	P					N	
d	P					N	
e	P					N	
f	P						N
g	P						N
h	P						N
i	P						N
j	P						N

a A seabird of North Atlantic coasts with a large coloured beak

b Fine yellow dust on the male part of a flower that causes other flowers to produce seeds when it is carried to them

c A large non-poisonous snake that kills small animals by crushing them

d An action of a court or ruler forgiving a person for an unlawful act

e A substance that harms or kills if an animal or plant takes it in

f A powerful or strong feeling

g A part separated or cut off

h A large water bird that eats fish, storing them in a pouch under its beak

i A regularly repeated arrangement with ornamental effect

j A black and white flightless swimming seabird, especially of the Antarctic

5 Place the ten list words in alphabetical order.

Did You Know?

6 At a circus all the action and fun takes place in the ring in
the big tent. The word *circus* means **ring** or **circle** The
Romans built large round stadiums where games and
races were held. These were called circuses because of
their shape. One large stadium was called the *Circus
Maximus* which means the biggest ring because it had
seats for 350,000 people. Today we call a circus the group
of people and animals that move from town to town,
instead of circus meaning the place where the show is
held.

Jumbled Words

7 Unjumble these list words.

llecgoe   osapteg
eghcan   grvlpeeii
aarvge   eeaagvr
egaruoc   ergeveba
egairram   gganee

Ring Word

8 Look at the letters below and see if you can find the 11-letter
word hiding there. Start anywhere, but use each letter once only
and move along the lines connecting the circles.

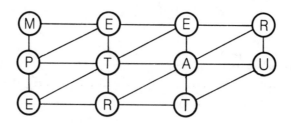

Unit 39

ew words

mild**ew**   st**ew**ard   sin**ew**   shr**ew**d   interv**iew**
pr**eview**   j**ew**el   n**ew**t   cash**ew**   sl**ew**

1   Write each of the list words in your book. Use each one in a sentence of your own.

Boxed Words

2   Two list words are jumbled up in each of the boxes below. What are the words? To help you, the <u>first</u> letter of one word and the <u>last</u> letter of the other word are circled.

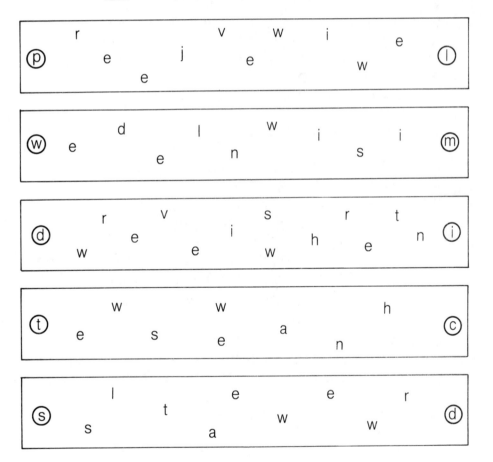

BO Words

3 Use the clues to find these words that all contain the letters **BO**.

a			B	O		
b			B	O		
c	B	O				
d	B	O				
e				B	O	
f			B	O		
g					B	O
h		B	O			
i				B	O	

a A man in charge of a monastery or abbey
b The joint in the middle of your arm
c To talk a lot about how good you are
d Past tense of "buy"
e Very tall grass with stiff hollow stems
f No one; no person
g A beautifully-coloured arch you can sometimes see in the sky
h To put an end to something
i Just born

Front and Back

4 Each of these words begins and ends with the same two letters. Use the clues to help you find the missing letters.

_ _ rmi _ _	A wood-eating insect
_ _ ca _ _	A period of ten years
_ _ gib _ _	Clear; easily read
_ _ sul _ _	Used in the treatment of diabetes
_ _ irteen _ _	An unlucky day if a Friday
_ _ co _ _	To work out a coded message
_ _ ma _ _	A red edible fruit
_ _ qui _ _	Need
_ _ bl _ _	A symbol; a special design

Name the City

5 Answer each of these clues. Then rearrange the first letters of each answer to make the name of a town in New Brunswick and Ontario.

a Someone who lives in the next house or nearby
b To become dry and lifeless; fade and shrivel
c A speech, either spoken or written
d A violent, destructive wind; a violent whirlwind
e Broad mouth of a river into which the tide flows
f To turn into vapour; remove water from
g Wood or coal partly burned but no longer flaming
h A furnace for melting ore in order to get metal out of it
i A garden plant with large crisp green leaves that are used for salad

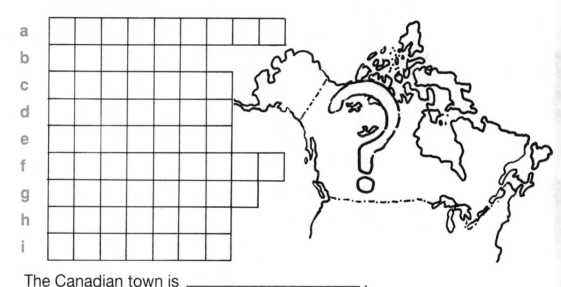

The Canadian town is _____ .

ent or ant

6 Complete these words by adding either **ent** or **ant**

tru ___ ___ ___   abs ___ ___ ___   differ ___ ___ ___
depend ___ ___ ___   consult ___ ___ ___   ten ___ ___ ___
observ ___ ___ ___   abund ___ ___ ___   confid ___ ___ ___
afflu ___ ___ ___   inst ___ ___ ___   expedi ___ ___ ___
extravag ___ ___ ___   assist ___ ___ ___   pres ___ ___ ___

Unit 40

Review

1 Choose the correct word.

a	catalog	cataloge	catalogue
b	teese	tease	teas
c	jamboore	jamboree	jamborey
d	proceed	procede	proseed
e	breakfast	breckfast	brekfirst
f	conceal	conseal	conceil
g	bycicle	bycycle	bicycle
h	center	senter	centre
i	desine	design	disign
j	persentage	percentage	percentige
k	postige	postege	postage
l	cashew	cashoo	cashwho
m	jool	jewle	jewel
n	vaige	vague	vage
o	referee	refeere	refferee
p	theater	theeter	theatre

2 Write these words into your book and group them into *word families*.

plague	reveal	gnash
nonsense	fleece	perform
coarse	tongue	college
marriage	pleasure	eerie
persuade	mildew	measure
morgue	course	exceed
accident	performance	gnat
newt	beverage	century
gnarled	science	slew

3 Find the small words that are in the larger words.

plague	appease	reindeer
measure	reveal	piece
permission	courage	percentage
mildew	steeple	sinew

Jumbled Words

4 Unjumble each word. Then write the plural for each word. The first one has been done for you.

a	leebt	beetle	beetles
b	unoteg	———	———
c	lewej	———	———
d	rehatte	———	———
e	bergevae	———	———
f	ulotacage	———	———
g	rytcuen	———	———
h	cenrorepfam	———	———
i	sing	———	———
j	lecciby	———	———
k	shacew	———	———
l	eexscu	———	———
m	rdnreeei	———	———

Mixed Words

5 Each group of letters contains two words from Units 31 to 39. What are the words?

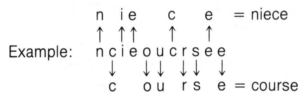

Example:

n i e c e = niece

n c i e o u c r s e e

c o u r s e = course

nsoinsleennsece
fpaetirgfueect
ceonncegalage
pprriovmiilseege
stsieenpleew

vpolruentveeirew
lreaegusiegn
erleceitrgicnity
dpecerrheaseaps
chnamepagwnet

A Jumbo Word Search

6 How many words from Units 31 to 39 can you find in this word search? The words go across the page and down the page.

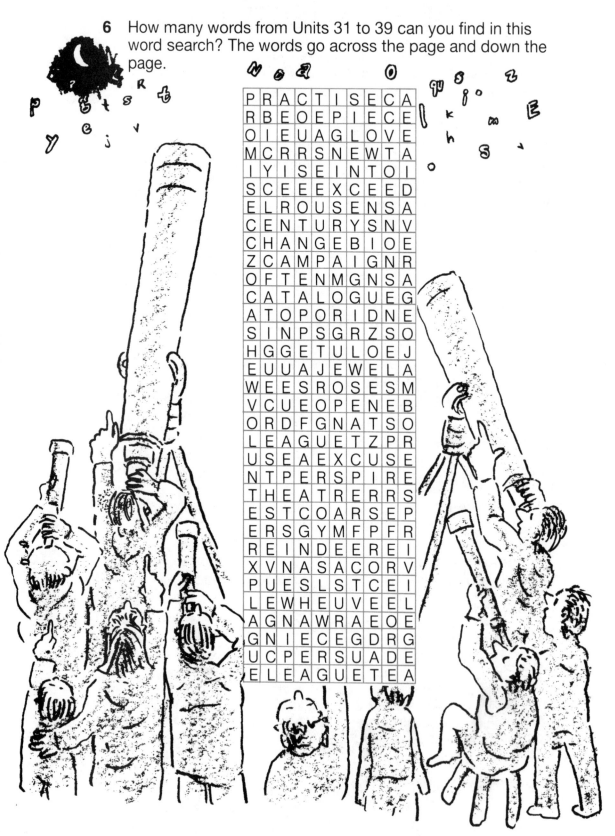

```
P R A C T I S E C A
R B E O E P I E C E
O I E U A G L O V E
M C R R S N E W T A
I Y I S E I N T O I
S C E E E X C E E D
E L R O U S E N S A
C E N T U R Y S N V
C H A N G E B I O E
Z C A M P A I G N R
O F T E N M G N S A
C A T A L O G U E G
A T O P O R I D N E
S I N P S G R Z S O
H G G E T U L O E J
E U U A J E W E L A
W E E S R O S E S M
V C U E O P E N E B
O R D F G N A T S O
L E A G U E T Z P R
U S E A E X C U S E
N T P E R S P I R E
T H E A T R E R R S
E S T C O A R S E P
E R S G Y M F P F R
R E I N D E E R E I
X V N A S A C O R V
P U E S L S T C E I
L E W H E U V E E L
A G N A W R A E O E
G N I E C E G D R G
U C P E R S U A D E
E L E A G U E T E A
```

List Words in This Book

a–e
decorate
celebrate
parade
climate
chocolate
replace
taste
waste
separate
language

e–e
scene
mere
stampede
hemisphere
complete
athlete
concrete
compete
sincere
recede

o–e
suppose
telescope
microscope
drone
zone
chrome
revoke
strove
cope
elope

i–e
decide
favourite
missile
admire
require
surprise
practise
practice

u–e
costume
produce
include
volume
salute
furniture
capsule
agriculture
parachute
treasure

ay
decay
payment
bayonet
dismay
portray
layer
prayer
array
repay
essay

y = 'e'
factory
century
especially
naughty
electricity
enemy
beauty
industry
library
secretary

qu
question
square
quarry
squash
mosquito
equator
quartz
quilt
mosque

or
history
factory
calculator
scissors
interior
orchestra
choral
refrigerator
radiator
monitor

messenger
whether
deserve
passenger
shoulder
saucer
exercise
different
dangerous
government

er
daughter
consider
minister
drawer
laughter
prisoner
recover
dessert
lantern

wh
whistle
whisper
whether
wharf
whine
whisker
whimper

ch	ss	soft 'g'	silent letters
handkerchief	guess	danger	guard
sandwich	success	imagine	guide
chocolate	scissors	college	science
character	business	general	scene
choir	necessary	pigeon	chemistry
machine	address	revenge	stomach
stomach	blossom	marriage	hymn
chemical	possible	genius	column
chose	message	manager	
chimney	massage	lounge	

ph	ie	le	ough
phrase	believe	possible	enough
physical	relief	whistle	plough
pharmacy	achieve	bicycle	bough
phantom	grief	terrible	drought
trophy	handkerchief	probable	cough
microphone	niece	responsible	though
sphere	piece	muscle	although
graph	pier	eagle	dough
dolphin	shield	cable	
prophet	shriek	article	

au	ei	ur	ui
autograph	receive	surround	bruise
audience	either	burst	cruise
author	neither	surface	suit
automatic	deceive	curtain	suite
authority	ceiling	surprise	nuisance
laundry	conceit	furniture	juice
launch	conceive	burglar	fruit
cautious	height	urgent	quiver
gauze	veil	surgeon	
exhausted	weigh	disturb	

ure	**y = 'i'**	**ar**	**ue**
torture	dye	collar	tongue
agriculture	lying	harbour	fatigue
pressure	supply	separate	plague
departure	pygmy	guard	synagogue
leisure	mystery	library	catalogue
fracture	rhythm	secretary	league
pasture	cygnet	harvest	vague
puncture	pyramid	similar	revue
enclosure	crystal	carnival	cue
signature	myth	vinegar	morgue

se	**ee**	**ea**	**soft 'c'**
promise	steeple	measure	silence
practise	referee	pleasant	decide
excuse	jamboree	pleasure	accident
course	fleece	breakfast	science
coarse	reindeer	league	century
tease	volunteer	decrease	bicycle
rouse	proceed	appeal	electricity
appease	exceed	theatre	centre
nonsense	eerie	reveal	niece
else	beetle	conceal	piece

silent 'g'	**ge**	**ew**	**per**
gnash	privilege	mildew	perform
gnaw	ravage	steward	performance
gnarled	beverage	sinew	perhaps
gnat	engage	shrewd	permission
sign	courage	interview	perfect
resign	postage	preview	percentage
campaign	average	jewel	perspire
reign	change	newt	persuade
design	college	cashew	
champagne	marriage	slew	